IRRESISTIBLY DRAWN TO THE EUCHARIST

Juan Gutiérrez González, M.Sp.S.

IRRESISTIBLY DRAWN TO THE EUCHARIST

CONCHITA CABRERA DE ARMIDA'S
most beautiful writings about the Eucharist

English translation by
MARK GUSCIN

ST PAULS

Alba
House

Originally published in Spanish under the title *Atracción irresistible por la Eucaristía* by San Pablo-Mexico (2000).

Library of Congress Cataloging-in-Publication Data

Conchita, 1862-1937.
    [Attración irresistible por la Eucaristía. English]
    Irresistibly drawn to the Eucharist : Conchita Cabrera de Armida's most beautiful writings about the Eucharist / English translation by Mark Guscin.
    p. cm.
    At head of title: Juan Gutiérrez González, M. Sp. S.
    Includes bibliographical references.
    ISBN 0-8189-0908-0 (alk. paper)
    1. Lord's Supper—Catholic Church. I. Gutiérrez González, Juan, 1935- II. Title.

BX2215.3 .C6613 2002
234'.163—dc21
                                   2002018691

Produced and designed in the United States of America by the Fathers and Brothers of the Society of St. Paul, 2187 Victory Boulevard, Staten Island, New York 10314-6603, as part of their communications apostolate.

ISBN: 0-8189-0908-0

Printing Information:

Current Printing - first digit   1   2   3   4   5   6   7   8   9   10

Year of Current Printing - first year shown

2002   2003   2004   2005   2006   2007   2008   2009   2010

TABLE OF CONTENTS

INTRODUCTION

This book offers the reader the most remarkable texts about the Eucharist written by a Mexican woman, who was married, had children and then became a widow. This woman was Concepción Cabrera de Armida, affectionately known as "Conchita." She passionately loved Jesus in the Holy Sacrament, to such a point that he became the center of her life.

The reader will quickly become aware of the prophetic nature of this spiritual experience, which thirty years after Vatican II proclaims the central mystery of the Christian faith.

Conchita describes in these texts her experience of the physical presence of Christ in the Eucharist. She also passes on the teachings she received from him, and recalls her mission in the bosom of the Church.

Conchita's pages about the Eucharist lead the reader into the heart of her spirituality and help us understand the depth of this secular woman's love for Jesus. They represent a privileged way into the writings of this great mystic, a gift of God for the Church of today. We use the word "mystic" in the sense explained by Fr. Juan Gutiérrez González, M.Sp.S., who has devoted many years to the theological study of Conchita's life and spirituality.[1] According to this Mexican theologian, the word de-

---

[1] Fr. Juan Gutiérrez González, M.Sp.S., was appointed by his congregation to study the theological aspects of the case for Concepción Cabrera de Armida's beatification in Rome. The texts in this book have been taken from the book written by this theologian, *Concepción Cabrera de Armida, Cruz de Jesús. Vida Mística e itinerario espiritual*, San Luis Potosí (published by La Cruz de Jesús María), 1998. We have

notes a person who is led by the Holy Spirit, putting into practice the Spirit's gifts. The Holy Spirit took over Conchita's soul
and she lived under this divine impulse, not in a human way but
rather as the Spirit wished. This Divine Spirit was not only the
driving force behind her soul's actions, but also her rule and cri-
teria for living. Conchita lived according to the gifts of the Holy
Spirit and experienced the divine influx of this Spirit. Fr Juan
Gutiérrez wrote the following about her:

"Conchita lives in the world, but as a mystic can and should.
She seeks penitence and humility, because she is a mystic. She
is not attached to the things of this world, because she is a mystic. She seeks solitude in the middle of a life in society with its
parties and entertainment, because God has filled her and, in a
profound union of knowledge and love, he has let her touch and
feel him. She desires the salvation of the entire world because
she has felt God's greatness so very close."[2]

It is this mystical life that allows Conchita Cabrera de
Armida to perceive, taste, love and desire God in such an extraordinary way in the Holy Sacrament of the altar. And it is in
this sense that we can say Concepción Cabrera de Armida is a
mystic of the Eucharist.

The first point we should make is that the Mexican personality and sensitivity of this woman are expressed in a style
that might confuse the reader, with its passionate raptures and
dramatic episodes. But let us not be mistaken about this. Simple
words repeated day after day give rise to the irradiation of a pres-

---

shown the textual reference in this book in brackets. Regarding the meaning of
the word "mystic," Fr. Gutiérrez refers us to Saint Thomas, for whom the essence
of the word lies in the fact that when in a mystical state, one's reason is not only
illuminated by faith, but one's soul is also driven to work under the impulse of the
gifts of the Holy Spirit.

[2] J. Gutiérrez González, M.Sp.S., *Una Mística en el interior de la Iglesia Madre*,
Madrid, (Ediciones Encuentro), 1991, pp. 7-19; cf. J. Gutiérrez González, M.Sp.S.
*Présente la grande Conchita. Écrits spirituels de Concepción Cabrera de Armida, Tome
I, De la naissance aux fiançailles spirituelles (1862–1894)*, Traduit de l'espagnol par
Dominique Reyre, Paris (François-Xavier de Guibert), 1999, pp. 9-24.

ence that illuminates and guides an ordinary life. These words spring spontaneously from a fascinated perception that seeks to express the inexpressible ... they were stammered out by a heart on fire, which as we have said, was consumed by passion for Jesus in the Eucharist.

And even if the reader tires of so much emotion, so much pouring out of the soul, by reading on he will find pearls whose beauty and theological depth will strengthen his faith and stir his intellect in the mystery of the Eucharist. Discovering aspects he did not know, or rediscovering what he thought he knew, seeing how fervently Conchita prepared herself to take Holy Communion, how she received Jesus and gave thanks, the reader will feel his love for the Eucharist grow.

His heart will become warm again from contact with the fire of these writings, and will be cured of the indifference and the thoughtlessness with which the world of today treats the Eucharist.

However, in order to understand these original writings, we have to place them in context, in the life and times of their author.

Wife, mother and writer

Concepción Cabrera de Armida was born into a rich and very large family on December 8th, 1862, in a province of the north of Mexico, in the city of San Luis Potosí. She was the seventh of twelve children. Her parents, Octaviano Cabrera Lacavex and Clara Arias y Rivera, had also been born in San Luis Potosí, and their parents were of Spanish blood who came from families of landowners. Conchita's grandmother on her mother's side owned no less than seven ranches. Conchita's education was rudimentary, since she spent most of her teenage years on horseback, visiting the ranches with her father. She loved music and singing, had a beautiful voice and could play the piano. She is said to have been exceptionally beautiful. She met her future husband, Francisco Armida, at one of the numerous balls organized by the high society of the city.

She was engaged to him at thirteen, and married him nine years later, when she was 22. They had nine children, and Conchita became a widow at 39.

This woman, who was a wife and mother, reached the heights of the mystical life. When she was 32 she received the grace of the mystical betrothal to Christ (1894),[3] and then at 45 she received the grace of the *Mystical Incarnation*.[4] However, she never neglected her marital, family and social duties. She carried out her housework and also obeyed the order from God, her spiritual advisor, to write down the teachings that she received daily in prayer.

Conchita thus wrote almost every day of her life[5] from when she was 31. Between 1893 and 1936, from when she was 31 up to when she was 75 (two months before her death), she wrote a diary (*Cuenta de conciencia*) consisting of 66 large notebooks, or 22,500 pages of intimate spiritual writings, in which she tells freely and openly what she had lived.

There are in this account pages that contain an admirable depth and great wealth about the mystery of the Eucharist, a real treasure for theologians. One small detail will suffice to show

---

[3] After burning the initials of Christ, JHS, onto her chest, as a sign of belonging and gift (January 14, 1894), Conchita was called to the *mystical betrothal*. A short time afterwards, she had a vision of the Cross of the Apostolate. At the same time, the founding of the Order of the Sisters of the Cross was announced, as was the future founding of the Missionaries of the Holy Spirit, whose founder was Fr. Félix de Jesús Rougier, in 1914.

[4] On March 25, 1906, after a lengthy preparation by the Lord involving great purifications, she lived the grace of the Mystical Incarnation. Fr. Juan Gutiérrez González, M.Sp.S., explains in depth the theological nature and foundation of this grace in the first volume of his above-mentioned work.

[5] 46 published works were presented in Rome for the process of her beatification. There were also 66 volumes of her diary, together with other works and 6227 letters, most of which were written to bishops, priests and family.

to what extent the Eucharist was a fundamental part of Conchita's personality and spirituality — in modesty and humility she never signed her writings with her name, preferring to state *"by the author of In Front of the Altar."*

A time of revolts and persecution

Conchita was born and lived in the Mexico of violent religious persecution and a markedly anti-Christian revolution. In the second half of the nineteenth century, there were no nuns left in Conchita's city, San Luis Potosí. President Benito Juarez's (1806–1872) liberal government had decreed by the *Reform Laws* the expropriation of the ranches (and so a large part of Conchita's family's estates were confiscated), and alarming measures against the Church.[6] Bishops had been exiled from 1859 on. On August 3rd, 1862 ecclesiastical chapters were suppressed, and on February 26th, 1863 religious communities were banished.

A very anticlerical atmosphere thus marked Conchita's youth. The nuns of the Sacred Heart, in charge of elementary education, were only able to return to San Luis Potosí in 1886, when they founded a community for schooling on the ruins of the old convent of Carmen.[7] This is why Conchita could not

---

[6] Cf. A. Alcalá Alvarado, M.Sp.S., *Historia general de la Iglesia en América Latina*, Mexico (Ediciones Paulinas), 1984, pp. 231-287. This book summarizes and synthesizes previous studies about the time in question. Cf. Velázquez Rodríguez Primo Feliciano, *Historia de San Luis Potosí*, 1982, Vol. I, pp. 57-69. A good picture of the sufferings undergone by priests and nuns in San Luis Potosí in these persecutions can be found in *Entorno Histórico de la infancia y adolescencia de la escritora mística Dña. Concepción Cabrera de Armida*, a presentation by R. Montejano y Aguiñaga, at the College of María Luisa Olanier in San Luis Potosí on March 3, 1987.

[7] The school was formally opened in 1892, cf. Velázquez Rodríguez Primo Feliciano, op. cit., pp. 121-123.

know about the consecrated life until two years after her marriage. This was without doubt one of the most painful experiences in her life, realizing that she could have belonged entirely to Jesus as a nun. But Divine providence had decided otherwise, and it was to a secular woman that God wished to entrust a mission within the bosom of the Church of the time. This mission consisted, while she was still in the world, of founding the Works of the Cross, in which there were two congregations of worshipers of the Most Holy Sacrament, one for women (the *Sisters of the Cross*) and the other for men (the *Missionaries of the Holy Spirit*). This could only be carried out in faith and obedience, since as we have already seen, the Church was suffering terrible persecutions. This led Conchita to say, when speaking about her project for God, that *"the Lord wishes his work to be founded on the agony of Mexico."*

The family's devotion to the Eucharist

Conchita's lifelong love for the Eucharist came first from her own family. Her father's mother was deeply devoted to the Holy Sacrament. She had founded the *Perpetual Vigil of the Holy Sacrament* in San Luis Potosí. As for Conchita's mother, she too felt a deep love for the Eucharist and imbued her daughter with this love and that of the Most Holy Virgin. Conchita recalls this when she writes, *"whenever she could, she would take us to see the Holy Sacrament"* (T. 22).

Her First Communion, a personal discovery of the Eucharist

It was in this fervent family atmosphere that Conchita took her First Holy Communion. This is how she describes receiving Jesus for the first time.
"I made my First Holy Communion on my tenth birthday, on

December 8th, 1872, the feast of the Immaculate Conception. I do not remember too much about it, because of my lack of enthusiasm and stupidity, just an immense pleasure inside and enjoying wearing a white dress. From that time on, my love for the Holy Eucharist grew constantly, and I would happily go to receive Communion. When I was 15 or 16, I was allowed to receive it 4 or 5 times a week, and shortly afterwards, every day.

I was happy, very happy *to receive Communion; it was an essential part of my life! How many time I received Communion the day after going to a dance or to the theater, so as not to feel stained!"* (T.12).

Her engagement and marriage did not weaken her love for the Eucharist

Conchita was engaged for nine years before marrying Francisco Armida, whom she calls Pancho. She taught him to receive Holy Communion as many times as possible, and never stopped praying for his soul from the start. This is how she explains how she loved both Pancho and Jesus.

"My engagement never made me feel that I belonged less to God, it was so easy to be both! When I was in bed alone, I thought of Pancho and then of the Eucharist, my great pleasure" (T.26).

Conchita adds that she would receive Communion as often as she could, saying *"I went to have Communion every day, and then to see him as he went by. My thoughts of Pancho never got in the way of my prayers. I would dress up and try to look nice just to please him, I would go to the theater and to balls just to see him, nothing else mattered. In the middle of all this, I never forgot my God; I remembered him almost always and was inexpressibly drawn to him. Many times I would wear a rough hair shirt underneath my silk dresses, which mattered to me as much as if they were made of sackcloth, enjoying the pain for my Jesus. As I said, I never saw this as sinful, and many times I would go to receive Communion* the day after, until I was told it was not correct to do this. This caused me great suffering" (T. 26).

When love for the Eucharist started filling her heart however, Conchita began to feel torn apart inside because of her obligations as a woman of the world. *"So many times a 'good night' would drag me away in tears from the school chapel, to get ready for a dinner or a dance and miss Communion, without being able to show my sorrow! I left my soul, torn apart, at the feet of the divine Child. My tears fell in the chapel, witness and partner to my pain"* (T.44).

Her husband's promise on their wedding day

On November 8th, 1884, Conchita married Francisco Armida. Conchita tells how he granted her two great favors — *"I remember at lunch time, when everybody was toasting us, etc., that I decided to ask my husband for two things, and he agreed to them. The first was to let me have Communion every day, and the second was not to be jealous. Poor thing! He was so good, so much so that many years later he would stay with the children while I went to church, and even in his last illness, before he lost consciousness, he would ask me if I had been to receive Our Lord. God will surely have rewarded him for this favor, which meant my life to me"* (T.35).

A note about this edition

There are so many eucharistic texts in Conchita's work that a book twice as long as this one would be needed to publish all of them. The aim of this book, however, is to give a general idea about Conchita's spirituality based on the Eucharist. In order to achieve this, we have followed the chronology of the main spiritual events that left their mark on the life of this woman. First of all, we have grouped together texts that illustrate the heart's desire Conchita felt for the Eucharist, and then those that describe the mystical experience of the physical presence of Jesus in the Host. The next group consists of the eucharistic teachings that Conchita received from Jesus himself (the divine words are in italics). Finally, in the last section, we have put together the texts that speak of the specifically eucharistic mission that Conchita had in the bosom of the Church.

May she be the spiritual mother of those who read this book, converting them into worshipers who seek the Father, *"real worshipers who worship the Father in spirit and in truth"* (John 4:23).

Dominique Reyre, Château de Festes, France, on the feast of Corpus Christi

1

IRRESISTIBLY DRAWN TO THE EUCHARIST

My heart's only happiness

How divine you are — you hold in your tabernacle all the delights of heaven that the world cannot appreciate. Oh my Jesus! I am humbled and confused before this incomprehensible mystery.

Only love — and what love! — has made you crush your holy heart to such an extent. That is where our soul's life resides, our heart's only happiness. Heart and soul of all virtues, you have them to share among those who come to you in good will. I am in ecstasy, I can go no further, my reason is lost and confused in such a deep mystery. But what can I say about the Eucharist? I can only feel... you never satisfy me, I receive you, I feel you filling my being, and yet I am never satisfied (T.54).

How can I not see in you, my Jesus, the object of my longing, if when I receive you in Communion I feel all my desires and wishes fulfilled? The world has never given me the divine well-being I feel in those moments. Yes, my Jesus, you and only you are capable of filling all the recesses of my heart. The soul's desires are infinite, and they can only be met by something infinite like you (T.55).

I cannot speak of the Eucharist

Holy Eucharist: sacred and immaculate Host that holds the Godhead itself, I cannot speak of you, yet the irresistible attraction on my whole being makes me break out sobbing, as only the tears of the soul can tell you what I feel. Oh! I see you in a transparent Host as material substance, but faith takes away the veil with which you cover yourself, love shaking the foundations of my heart makes me feel your presence, and the joy you cause it to feel lifts it up to the sublime hope of possessing you, overcoming all the obstacles that separate us. Oh Lord! I will pass away, generations will come and go, and only you, *you*, will never pass away. When you end your mission of charity on earth, you will keep on giving yourself forever in heaven to the hearts that belong to you... let me be one of them, Lord, please (T.75).

My soul leaves me behind

For some time now, when I am in front of the Blessed Sacrament, I have been feeling something extraordinary in my soul, something I did not feel often in the past. My soul leaves me, and I cannot think, pray or do anything at all with my understanding. Only every now and then, almost without thinking about it, I manage to express the aspirations of my heart. Following your advice, I now try to place my soul in the Sacred Heart of Jesus (T.123).

Hierognosis[8]

During Mass, I often sense the moment when Jesus Christ comes down into the hands of the priest, although I do not see

---

[8] This phenomenon is known by theologians as *hierognosis*, or "knowledge of the

it. I cannot explain it, but a movement or feeling inside announces the moment, and I have confirmed it when the Host is exposed and the little bell is not rung. In front of the physical presence of Jesus in the Eucharist I feel a very peculiar and inexplicable attraction (T.123). Sometimes, I suddenly feel Jesus drawing near, and even if I am far away, I run to the window or to the door to see for myself, and there he is... and in a state of confusion, I adore and thank him. This happens when Communion is taken to a sick person.

Once when this happened, nobody was coming and yet I clearly felt him coming near. And lo and behold, he must have been coming out of the tabernacle because some moments later he passed by, near me. When I let my feeling guide me, I have known on which altar he is, even in churches I had never been in before. In one church where I used to go regularly, I went up to the tabernacle and felt a great sense of emptiness. I did not know what was happening until I looked closer and realized that they had taken the Hosts to another altar. Jesus is so good to this wretched person!

Many times, when I was in a city I did not know, at night on a tram, on any number of streets, this feeling in my heart came upon me, and on several occasions a very good and holy friend who was with me would remark, "We are very near such and such a church." I was overwhelmed and moved on seeing the grace of Jesus, and I adored him with all the love of my poor soul.

Once I felt that Jesus was present in a tabernacle where he did not usually dwell. I was told he was not there but inside I knew he was. A priest happened to pass by and told us all to kneel down because the monstrance was there. I could not hold back my tears on this occasion, and resting my forehead behind the tabernacle I felt an incomparable joy and I cried my heart out, all his, so close to Jesus' ears.

---

holy." Some mystics have received the gift of being able to identify the sacred presence of the Host at a distance.

On another occasion, the lamp on the altar was lit. Those who were with me were convinced he was there, but my heart told me he was not. I went to find out and we asked the sacristan, who affirmed what I had been thinking. Jesus was not there. Of course, nobody understood anything about what was happening to me. These things that have been happening make me feel embarrassed and overwhelmed, and endlessly thankful.

There are however moments when this makes me feel so good that I am afraid of becoming vain. Sometimes I tell myself not to think about it, but then it happens again and my soul is filled with this pleasure. Sometimes I am wrong about it, and I am happy that God lets this happen to humble me, but most of the time it is the opposite (T.124).

During Communion

During Communion I very clearly feel Jesus coming... he covers himself, coming down, hiding himself so as not to dazzle me. Oh Father! I cannot help being moved when this moment arrives. I love the Holy Eucharist so much... it has done me such good! It is my support, my breath, my life, my strength! I would die without this divine breath... it is indispensable to me for my time on earth and for my arrival in heaven (T.124).

My place is by your side

Oh Jesus, I love you so much in the Sacrament of your love! My place is there, by your side, and on the nights when I do not visit you, when you do not warm this poor soul, it is weak, cold, downcast and sad.... I love it when everyone goes away and I draw near to Jesus alone... to relieve my heart... to ask for so many things, and to listen to him.... Oh, yes! To listen to him...! And how very much the Heart of Jesus, burning with love for us, has to say to our souls which are so ungrateful, selfish and vile! (T.124).

And suddenly, my wounded soul leaps with holy joy at a very vivid impression. I am jolted by a sudden sensation, and then I see that just then the tabernacle had been opened and he was letting me know, as I had not seen it. I felt the physical presence of the Lord before receiving him.

My God! How could anyone doubt this clear mystery? (T.132).

During Mass

During Mass, more than in other religious services, I feel overcome, I do not know how, I cannot explain it. A divine attraction that is not under my control draws me towards the altar, especially during the Consecration. I feel the physical presence of Jesus Christ some times more than others, in such a way that I cannot doubt it, and I see apart from faith and separate from other feelings (T.138).

How is it possible!

My God! How is it possible that consuming such a great fire daily, we can be lukewarm... frozen and hard as granite? How can this absurdity be, an enigma that I am not capable of solving? Why are we not turned into ash? I cannot understand it! (T.194).

My intellect is powerless

Oh Jesus! Oh Eucharist! What would become of us without it, Father? Why can nothing else come to the heart in love each dawn as a Sacrament? Why must we suffer so many hours of absence, in solitude without the Beloved? When will we be able to possess him forever and endlessly, for all eternity? What will that be like? Oh my God! I lose my power of reasoning... my soul faints when I contemplate Jesus... heaven's heaven... that heart of love and pain... in the presence of the infinite and incomprehensible Godhead (T.203).

Continuously driven to the Eucharist

What can I say about my beloved Eucharist, except that it is my life, my breath, my hope, my love, my purity and my everything? Oh Father, when I speak of this divine Sacrament, I do not know where to begin or where to end, there are so many favors I owe it! (T.1170).

The desire to make amends

I did not want to go to bed without thinking of my Child of Bethlehem, and of my Jesus in the Eucharist... oh! and how wearisome the time left before receiving him seemed.

What a *hunger* for Jesus, what *thirst* for his blood and his tears!... I can still feel in my poor heart the living desire to make amends with my life, blood, sacrifices and everything I have for priests' sins that terrify me so... I really shudder at the idea, more than the idea, at the horrible reality of the sinful way they treat him on the altar. And, my Jesus, you suffer all this in silence... Oh Father of my soul! What can I do? (T.350).

The Eucharist attracts my soul

Yesterday afternoon I ran with great yearning to where the Blessed Sacrament was exposed. *The divine Eucharist is a magnet for my soul* and I am happy when I am close to it, I lack nothing and I feel satisfied with everything, just like a child in his mother's arms (T.364).

A constant force that draws me to the Eucharist

December 4th, 1895. My soul is suffering great sadness and desolation. But I do not want to fall or faint in the fight even if it lasts until I die. Furthermore, in spite of the desolation which overcomes me, in the depths of my spirit I feel a constant force that draws me to cling to God, tending always, or almost always, to the Holy Eucharist; everywhere, at night, during the day, I feel this divine attraction in the very depths of my soul.

I am frozen in the upper part of my spirit, and yet inside an everlasting fire is burning, a fire that never goes out. I have suffered a sadness whose weight has made me shed abundant tears; I have not been able to control myself especially in front of my adorable Eucharist (T.561).

I offer him everything

Sorrows, setbacks, disappointments, much misery to lament over creatures who make life bitter... let it all be for God, *and may he support us and all our works.* I clearly see the all-powerful hand of God and his cooperation in everything, in all that happens, and it is admirable.... I feel very sensibly a loving confidence in Jesus. The Holy Eucharist draws me irresistibly....

I can also feel the struggle with the devil, his temptations to vanity, pride, anger, that strike my soul like lightning, yet thanks to God I think they do not stain it. I feel very clearly the struggle between the two spirits in my soul. This tug of war in my soul never leaves me, this pull, I would say, to that Center, that Magnet, love's Repose, God (T.692).

If only we knew!

If I could speak in the tongue of the seraphim, I would do so only to speak of this Sacrament of the most sublime love... of Jesus' love, based on sacrifice!... If only we understood something of what this adored Eucharist means for us! If only I could receive it sacramentally in my miserable breast every moment of the day! Make me love him, Father, with all the strength of my soul, and not to wish, think or feel anything except Jesus in the sacrifice of the Sacrament. I will gladly speak of him forever....

And who would believe it? After the fire that was burning in my soul upon receiving him, straight after and during all my prayer I was as cold as ice. Blessed be the Lord!

These sudden changes sometimes affect me, and I do not know why; it is probably my own fault. I also sometimes feel more ardent out of church, whereas prayer time seems to be marked by dryness (T.693).

Hunger for the Eucharist in the theater

While in the theater I was overcome by an extraordinary hunger for my eucharistic Jesus... alive... and my spirit sighed, longing to receive him. I feel an overwhelming tendency to fly to it, or better, to get closer to my Jesus, I know not in what intimate and absolute way.

I am drawn by this divine attraction... it is as if I were the

8

air and the Lord absorbed me or breathed me in... I cannot find the words to explain it... but my spirit, my thought and my will are destined to be there, as if they were nowhere else, in its center. If I could only faithfully translate the feelings of my soul and write them down! But unfortunately there is no dictionary in this world, no language suitable for making myself understood as I would wish. These things can be understood only by treading the same path (T.719).

I wish to give him souls

Poor Jesus in my adorable Eucharist! Father of mine, what can I do to console him? I wish to give him souls, many souls to glorify him, and I know not how. I want to see the divine and precious Dove honored, invoked and loved in a very special way, and the eternal Father to whom we owe so much... (T.926).

A very happy afternoon

I had a very happy afternoon yesterday, near, very near my Jesus Eucharist, praising him in the midst of the souls consecrated to him in his Oasis. My spirit was longing for his blessed company, and my heart was drawing me to the tabernacle.... After he had been placed on his throne, my breast was all choked up in the holy emotion of praise... joy... and gratitude.... When the Trisagion was sung, I do not know what great joy I felt inside when I heard the praises of the blessed Trinity.... My soul was swollen with holy jubilation in the procession since I was so near his adorable Eucharist.

I couldn't take my eyes off it. During the *Te Deum*... oh my God, how wonderful! My tears were running down, and the Lord was speaking to my heart... (T.1024).

I am jealous of the sacristans

Neither noise nor people nor the busy street are enough to take my mind off this Jesus I am contemplating without knowing how or why. My heart is still on fire, wounded, broken with a constant grief, loving and painful, that draws it to the Eucharist.... What would I not give to live at the foot of the tabernacle! I am jealous of the sacristans, the candlesticks, whatever draws near or is next to the tabernacle (T.1056).

From one church to another

In church today, my restless heart would not let me alone until I agreed to go to another church where the Host was exposed. I was content then in this divine presence of my adorable Eucharist that I never tire of looking at, amazed and overwhelmed by a holy impression that cannot be explained with words.

I sense, Father, that Jesus Christ, God and Man, is really and truly there, with all his perfection and attributes.... that the most blessed Trinity, realizing the greatest of all miracles, is enclosed within the tiny circle or tip of a consecrated wafer. It is his love that overwhelms me there, more than his might and endless power (T.1066).

I feel the presence of God in the Eucharist

Peace and continued longing for the divine Eucharist. After I go into a church, my heart leaps within my breast and beats faster, as if it wanted to leave its place and leap into the holy tabernacle. I feel with such sincerity and such certainty that God is there, I do not know how to explain it. His divine presence overwhelms me, it seems to call me, it tells me to draw near to him, to speak to him, to make requests, to love him deeply....

There takes place those conversations in which he gives himself to my soul and communicates with it with his grace, with the touch and comfort of the divine Dove. I think that if I could open that little door, my anguish, I would doubtless see him as he really is, with no sacramental veils. When my eyes see the sacred Host, something like a gentle and divine electric shock runs through me, at the same time strong and devouring, which leads me to unite myself, to embrace and draw closer to my God!

This is how the refuse and scum of the world, Father, rise up to the King of heaven, Christ Jesus, my adorable Eucharist. Oh Father! That I may love greatly this Sacrament of love and bring other souls to love it. Jesus wants them to live through him and for him, dead to everything that is not God (T.1070).

I want to see you, Lord

"When will I see you, Lord?" I said, "so I can be sure that what has happened to me is from you?" *"Your life is faith"* he answered and this is what I understood.

"But I want to see you, Lord," I insisted. *"You are looking at me"* he said, and I felt the physical presence of Jesus Christ visible in the monstrance, and I fell down on my knees before such great majesty, knowing for certain what was there, and I pleaded, I begged, I emptied my oppressed heart asking that if I were to be vain, I never wanted to see it in this life, since I shudder at the very hint of pride (T.1120).

Becoming a Host

The Eucharist is my life, and how I would like to receive it not only every day, every hour, every minute, but with every breath and heartbeat. I wish to merge with it, be as *white* as it is, to be the *Host*… all, all purity and sacrifice.

I cannot stand in front of the tabernacle without being in pain. This has happened to me since I was a little girl. The Lord asks it of me. I never tire of being with him; this need grows daily in my soul (T.1977).

Preparing myself to receive the Host

How I receive it. I draw near with my soul, Father, from the moment when I wake up. I call out for it with my lips, I attract it with my sighs, I long for it, I love it, and with a thousand acts of discipline I prepare this miserable and foolish body for it. My veins are torn, providing me every morning with fresh blood to offer him. My chalice is full to the brim with this lowly blood, drawn and extracted *out of love* to mingle with his blood on the altar, my Immaculate Lamb, and together they are offered up to God's throne, asking for grace.

Is it not an undeserved happiness and favor to have an altar, an Oasis, and the freedom to be able to do this for my Jesus without anybody knowing? My soul's blood, its life fluid, is also for Jesus. Power, feelings, and my life, I place them all at the foot of the tabernacle.

And the minutes fly by, reverberating in my heart, longing for the heavenly moment when the tabernacle opens and the holy form can be seen. It is so white, so bright, I observe it so pure and holy, trembling in the priest's hands! My heart opens like the poor rose and longs for dew from heaven. And of course, Jesus is the dew, a refreshing dew, a strengthening dew that gives it vigor, warmth, aroma and life!

I could not live without this sap of the Sacrament of love... the blood of my beloved is the lifeblood of my existence. What would I be without a consecrated Host? What indeed, without the holy breath that purifies me, inflames me, absorbs all my being and by consuming me gives me life? This is how I receive my beloved, but it is little, it is nothing, it is imperfect. It is cold, it is nothing compared to what he deserves. What shall I do, what shall I do?

If only I could be a seraphim, to offer him his burning ardor! If I could even be a martyr, to give him everything he is! If only I could be a cloudless sky to receive him! If only I possessed the purity of the angels to shelter him! If only I had the innocence of Mary and the feelings of her Immaculate Heart to envelop him! If only I had all the tenderness of every mother to caress him! Finally, if only I could be a *living Cross*, so he could be nailed to me and there remain forever!

But what can I offer him, Father Bernard, except poverty, ruin, darkness, cold, baseness and an abundance of misery? Oh Jesus, my Jesus Eucharist, sun of my existence, good of my life, my God, my only one, my everything! What can I say to you, what can I give you?... *I will tell you*, I am not worthy to receive you, and I will give you yourself, this Word that throbs within my soul! (T.1294).

My soul flies to the Eucharist

As soon as I see the Host exposed, it is as if my soul flies to him and adheres to him like the light to the sun. I care nothing for people and things, only he shines in the depths of my soul dimming everything and playing the divine chord of his love in all my being (T.3055).

2

THE MYSTICAL EXPERIENCE OF
THE PHYSICAL PRESENCE OF JESUS

Intense happiness

Today is Sunday and after I had just received Communion I had a beautiful thought, or rather it was the effect of the Communion that I can still feel and that makes me unspeakably happy.

Jesus came into me... but on feeling that the space was so little, he swelled up and spread out, so to say, and came out through all the pores of my body, more and more, I do not know to what extent... enveloping me, filling with light a space I cannot measure. Oh what a divine happening. I know not how I understood and felt it! I felt, Father, of course! very little, like a little dot, and he was no longer inside me, although he still filled me, and I was *lost in him*... up, down, Jesus everywhere, in an atmosphere of Jesus.... Oh God of my soul! I cannot explain any more, but you understand me!

Oh Jesus, Jesus, Jesus!... I cannot say any more and I can hardly hold the pen from emotion! (T.144).

Participation in the desolation of Jesus-Eucharist

I am extremely disappointed both inside and out, a disappointment never felt before, and I can find no consolation, neither human nor divine. I can feel nothing except this inexplicable internal pain that tortures and exhausts me. I would shout, but where? I would run but I have no strength. I would weep, my God, weep, but I cannot.

I would not flee, however, from this anxiety or helplessness even if I could, because I know it is your will, my Jesus. This is the only thing that gives me life.

Lord, for all my sins, so many, so very many... and for the sacrilege and insults to the Eucharist. Oh Lord! How can I wish to be consoled when you are sad? and how can I wish for relief if you are disconsolate, helpless, oh my Crucified One...! Just one look to strengthen me and give me life... (T.191).

The helplessness is still with me. After Communion today I felt Jesus come and fill me... but it was a sad Jesus who filled my soul, a Jesus in pain.... Is this possible? I have seen and felt Jesus as the dawn, as light, happiness... but full of sorrow and anxiety, communicating this to my soul, this had never happened to me. Luckily my spirit had some rest, not really rest but rather a painful immersion as participation with the Beloved.

The sadness and profound sorrow I still have were not caused by the devil, since I feel its divine origin, even if it is most bitter. Is there such a thing as shared desolation? (T.406).

Immense spaces

Once in a dreamlike state I understood this mystery. I saw very clearly how Jesus was wholly and truly inside the Host. It was like looking through the glass of a monocle which, though small, when held up reveals things greatly enlarged. Jesus Christ was wholly and completely there inside, with all his attributes and immense majesty. His sacred humanity was glorified in its natural size, but his divinity was incomprehensible. I do not know how I saw this. I understood it but cannot explain it.

The taste and fragrance of God

I do not wish to deceive, Father, but today the material taste of the Sacrament had a divine, delicate, and extraordinary flavor and fragrance. This surprised me as I had not experienced this before… what could that blood taste like, that white lily formed inside the most pure Mary? How delicate! What a stainless lily!

Do not think, Father, that I am exaggerating or looking for effect in my writing. This is not my intention, I only say what I feel but I cannot say how I feel it. It is not poetry or nonsense… What could be more poetic than Jesus! Nor is it my way of being, *dry* and cold, that tends to those things. I do not know how to use them either, but when I feel Jesus, or deal with things concerning him… everything else seems hard, prosaic, I do not know. This is why I search for harmony, light, flowers, aromas, because he is the center of all this and of all we see, a flimsy shadow of the hidden treasure, light from light, God from God… Jesus, Jesus, Jesus and everything is enclosed within Jesus. Oh Father, my heart is bursting! (T.224.a)

I felt this delicious *taste* again one day in Communion, but not so long nor so marked. I am so surprised by this Father! I knew nothing about it and had not even heard of it. I suspected that spiritual hunger and taste existed in the Holy Eucharist, but this taste, mystical-material, I do not know what to call it, I had never even imagined it. The Host had always tasted like a flour wafer, even when my Communion was most fervent, but this strange occurrence — may it be real — has astonished me. I know that you have tasted Jesus in this way, but please tell me if there

17

are any books about this, what it is and what it is called. Oh! what can heaven taste of if not heaven? These marvelous things, Father, leave me beside myself (T.260.d).

For the last few days when I receive Holy Communion, apart from that divine effect filling my soul, the Host has a material and perceptible taste, so delicate that I cannot explain it, but it joins together with the spiritual, producing an insatiable hunger for that divine element. These are the effects of the pure flesh of the Lord (T.1045).

Something new happened today that astonished me, and no matter how long I seek for natural explanations I cannot find any. In receiving Communion, I noticed that the sacred Host had an aromatic taste and smell like flowers or delicate perfume that remained until I swallowed it. How strange! I thought that it must have come from the priest's hands, but he does not use perfume and he had just received Communion and rinsed his fingers. My soul felt inexplicably well, a delicate freshness, something incomprehensible, and then it occurred to me to ask the Lord:

"What is this, my Jesus?" I then heard that sweet voice that deep down inside was saying to me, "*Am I not your white lily?*"

I remembered with shame that I had said that to him, and that I say in my acts of love and devotion, "Jesus, my Jesus, blood-stained lily, pure, innocent and nailed to a Cross for me…," and then I understood the reason for this taste of flowers and for this aroma and I said to him, full of surprise, "But is this possible, Lord?" "*What is not possible for me?*" he answered, and then I quickly expressed my love and endless gratitude (T.1473)

Jesus' suffering in the Eucharist

I felt fine at morning prayer, but what Jesus told me he suffers on his altars caused me great pain. Is it possible, Father, for Jesus to suffer where he should be adored, and *because of his own people*? And can one dare to complain? If only I could atone

18

for this offense! You can atone, Father, much better than I can, and in a thousand ways... it breaks my heart, and I see Jesus crying, crying.

"*Look*", he said to me, "*my tears fall, they run down onto these stones and move them... and the people for whom they well up in my soul despise them!*" (T.247).

This Jesus, Father! What can I do, not to reimburse him because that is impossible, but to thank him, yes, to thank him for the flood of grace that you have told me about and that I feel?

Jesus said to me, "*When people come to visit my tabernacle, I want them to dry my tears* every day, *wiping my eyes with their hearts*" (T.248). I long to suffer with Christ in pain.... I wish to be broken when Christ is broken... tears... *internal* sorrow for so much sorrow that Christ suffered for me, and suffers mystically in the Sacrament.

I see how the Godhead hides... and lets the Holy Humanity suffer so cruelly. And how all of him suffers... *and wishes to suffer...* for me. And I look at him in love, so cruel to himself... and so loving to me... and I see him, how even now in this adorable Sacrament he could destroy his enemies and yet he does not do so .. he is scorned a thousand times and suffers countless humiliations...

Heaven of my soul, Jesus Eucharist of my life! Come to my soul nailed to the Cross, I want to be nailed to the other side... (T.1508).

Piercing

After Communion and having swallowed the wafer, it was as if a sword went right through me, from my heart to my back; not really through my heart, although this too hurt, but rather from my left side to my back. The pain was not natural, and it was so intense that I could not breathe and my arms lost feeling, especially the left one, which has not yet recovered. What can this be? Desolation, helplessness, or an imitation of my Jesus' lance wound? As I have asked for the latter, I would not be surprised if it were this, the pain is perceptible-loving-dreadful, you understand me, Father (T.261.a).

Everything happened at once today, receiving Communion and feeling transfixed like yesterday, pierced by an intense pain both inside and out, the kind of pain that exhausts you. It is inside the spirit, because you want to express it by sighing and yet this does not relieve you, and it is grief, distress and pain that makes you moan even if you do not want to, at least people like me who do not know how to suffer much. This lasted a while with no consolation. Could it be, Father, that Jesus has heard me and from now on will be for me a lance that pierces me? Look how stupid, I tried to think of something else and rest for a few minutes, but the thought brought me back to myself, the gathering together of my thoughts drew me in and straight away the pain penetrated me.

This pain, Father, goes through all my body, and takes all feeling out of my arms. And then suddenly it disappears just like that, as if by magic. God's presence is very powerful (T.262).

When God embraces me

Listen, Father, when the time for going to the tabernacle draws near, my soul grows restless at night. It finds no place to be content and hurries me on to Jesus. As soon as it sees the poor little house in the distance, it leaves me and runs to the arms of its Beloved. It does not matter that the doors are closed, for what frontiers can exist when you are in love?

Sometimes it seems to leave me alone, and we are two different beings, and it is very strange. My poor heart is left here beating, my body is useless, and my soul is full of great joy... if you only knew how difficult it is to pull it back from there... a few more minutes... just a few kisses for Jesus... I still need my spiritual Communion... just another little look please, a few hugs, and he will tell me that he will stay there, or go home with me... and the minutes go by, my obligations call me and I have to get serious with this soul in love and drag it back, in spite of this useless rubbish, an awful receptacle for such a beautiful thing (T.271).

I think that the Lord is preparing me for something unknown. Today I felt his physical presence at Communion and a certain closeness with him, in interior intimacy. I cannot separate my spirit from him, even though my thoughts sometimes wander off to things of this world. Father, I can feel the pain of this internal piercing, sensitive and painful and I cannot rest from the sighs that well up in my soul. These are not flattering remarks or tender words for my God, Father, for my adorable Jesus... for my precious Dove... for anybody in the world. They are just to take me deeper into an interior peace, where I can hear soundless voices... divine melodies in an unknown language, ineffable utterings that purify the senses of the soul... enchanting them and taking them to ecstasy.

There and only there, Father, can my weary and suffering soul find rest. That is where you can hear the divine heart beating... where you can feel the joy of the Cross, far, very far from this earth... I understand without trying that these are the sweetest *areas* promised for the Oasis... and for a purpose; the afternoon when Jesus called me to the tabernacle he told me about these areas in his loving heart where the soul flies hidden within the Cross that pierces it (T.647).

God's tenderness

At Communion time, I experienced the physical presence of Jesus stronger than ever before.... I was feeling a little agitated and completely helpless but with great fervor too.... It seemed, my God, as if I were not on this earth!

21

At the same time I felt something very strange, a sense of love for all peoples, a mixture of pity, love and a desire to forgive all their failings. It was so strange, Father! My heart had never felt like that!

As a consequence or result of these clear feelings, divine peace then flooded my soul, submerging it in an immensity... of intimate pleasure... peaceful, rested, enveloped in and full of God alone, loving all souls (T.481).

All my eternity

Once again I experienced that living and vivid internal feeling for my adorable Eucharist. When my eyes were closed I felt him coming near and then leaving... on receiving Communion.

Oh my adorable Eucharist, I love you so much! You are my life... my eternity is right there in that little white circle, the divine Heart's nest... the Holy Trinity, heaven (T.540.d).

The purification of material things

A most extraordinary thing happened to me yesterday after Communion. I can still feel its effects throughout my body.

Anyway, after Communion, I clearly felt, oh God, how wonderful! the Lord physically present in my sensitive heart, and at the same time it was as if he were growing, growing within me, expanding or becoming larger, till he came out through all my body, as it were. This extraordinary feeling left me in suspense.

It was as if I had received the sun instead of the wafer and its rays were transfixing me. This seems like a very good comparison, because it really felt like my whole body was being transfixed by rays of light, from a warm light, from a Life-Light.

This was so clearly perceived by my spirit that I even

thought the people who were walking near me were going to disturb or damage the rays. This did not happen however — they went through them like one goes through a ray of sunlight, without touching or affecting them at all. How wonderful, how wonderful! Not only, Father, did I feel bathed in divinity, or absorbed in it, or attached to it... it was more than that, and this enrapturement grew and, I am embarrassed to admit it, I felt as if I were absorbed or assimilated into the Godhead itself.

I understood that God could not become me, i.e. with my malice, poverty, weakness and sin, and that was precisely why in an act of great kindness he lifted me up in a way to union with him... but this union was so high, so sublime and I had never felt it before. God was in me, and it was as if I had been turned into him. I am darkness, but I had been flooded and pierced with light, I was ice and yet I was burning with love like the Seraphim. I was *possessed* by God himself through my adorable Eucharist, and with God's own clarity I understood my own helplessness and nothingness and this loving God's power and goodness towards this vile and miserable piece of clay.

I could clearly see his beauty and my own ugliness... and the infinite wealth of graces stored up in the holy heart of Jesus... I was humbled and crushed before this great manifestation of goodness, I was sinking in my own misery... but, oh wonderful effect! just where I bowed my poor spirit down, the eternal majesty of my God also bowed down with me. If I went up, it seemed like the Lord went up with me, and if I went down, it seemed like he came down with me, like two things that have been fused together and cannot be separated.

I could still feel him here and there outside me, transfixing this vile body. Then I heard Jesus' voice say to me, "*See, my daughter, what is happening to you is material purification*" (this was in the Church of the Tabernacle of Mexico, near where one receives Communion). I understood that by purification he meant cleansing, and I said, "I am clean, my Jesus, because I have washed and bathed. What is this material purification by light and by Spirit? Does the Spirit purify matter, Jesus? Tell me because I do not understand." Jesus did not answer me and, even though I thought about it a lot, I did not manage to understand it.

The next day I said to him

"Tell me Jesus, why can I feel you so transparent within me, as if I were glass filled with your light and your rays went right through me, whereas I am clay and not glass, mud and a marsh, my Jesus, because this is what I touch and feel? Tell me, why does this happen to me?"

He answered me thus, *"The sun does not only go through glass, but also through mud and marshes, purifying them and drying them. Let it be, my daughter, you are my mud and everything that is of my will."*

I was overwhelmed and on this day of such great grace I said to Jesus, "Why me Lord? This confuses and dumbfounds me."

"Oh my daughter!" I recall him, being moved, saying, *"I fill what is empty, I help the weak who commit themselves into my hands, I am the Strength of the feeble, the Wealth of the poor, the Light of those who are blind to external things. I never come in this way to those who think they do not need me. Union is what I ask of your soul, my daughter, union"* (T.555).

I have felt saturated with my God from that day on, this holy and divine effect is lasting… the rays of light are no longer there externally, since they only lasted for a time, and yet my body feels again and again the lifeblood, the warmth, the energy and at the same time the peace, the blast of fire that went through it. Yes, it is in just this way, as if the divine wind still blows, that these strange things happen to me!

However, given that matter is so much less than the spirit, it is weakened and faints under these celestial forces. The earth cannot contain the heavens, and for that reason I say that the body is weak and can scarcely cope with supernatural life, and it would die, yes, this poor material would die if grace did not sustain it.

Oh Father, my Father! This poor clay vessel can hardly cope with the immensity of the soul joined to God! When will this prison be broken, when will this body finally disintegrate in honor of its Creator so that the spirit can take flight to its place, God, from where nobody will be able to separate it? I want to see my God... I can catch a glimpse of him... I can almost touch him, but there is a veil that I cannot tear, and my beloved Jesus shows through it, and that veil is my life, my breath, my existence, my only happiness on this earth. Oh adorable Eucharist! Beloved today more than ever of this miserable breast where you live (T.556).

I enter into God

After Communion today I felt the physical presence of the Lord inside me. It is an inexplicable thing, Father. I feel that I enter into him when he enters me, that I am lost in an ocean of light, in an abyss of greatness.... I could almost say that I feel the destruction of my own being, taking on at times another existence, another life, the life and existence of him who is the center of life, God and Life!

This cannot be understood and yet I feel it happen immediately on receiving Jesus in the Eucharist. I perceive the real presence of the Man-God wrapped in the thin veil of the bread... as if he were holding back his splendor so as not to dazzle me, and yet when I receive him, the mystery seems to be unveiled, and I would say that the immense Lord spreads out and swallows me up in the endless ocean of his immensity.

I understand, I do not know how, that God is present, wholly as God and man in any part of the consecrated Host, as in the whole wafer, as in all the Hosts put together, in all the ciboriums in the world. I cannot explain it but I see it clearly in my understanding and I feel it in my heart, as if it were by divine intuition, apart from faith. How wonderful, my God, blessed art thou! (T.616).

Absorbed by the immensity of God

I was fortunate enough to descend to *my* nothingness and to understand how the immensity of God absorbs this miserable atom of the earth… how the consecrated Host holds this immensity… and yet is so small, and how when we receive Communion and the holy wafer enters into us, we enter into it by a kind of divine transformation… absorbed, I would say, by the Godhead itself.

What great mysteries, Father, take place between God and the soul in this august Sacrament of love! Oh my God of Charity! Here, I think I see a gleam of your light to glimpse your great love for mankind! But will I ever be able to explain this in words? No, I can only feel, feel and adore you with the silent language of the soul that only You understand!

Why, Father, is the Eucharist not sufficiently known or loved? At least we will love it forever with all the strength of our souls, and sacrifice ourselves for it, won't we, Father? (T.627).

Offering the emptiness of the soul

Today I felt very cold before Communion and I had to make an effort to call my Jesus. What a remarkable mirror he is, Father, in which I can clearly see my own ineptitude, uselessness and poverty! I can indeed be a shining mirror of these things! I started to think then of *my emptiness*, offering this dunghill to the Lord because I do not have anything else. I do wish to be his forever even though I am nothing more than a poisonous spider, happily and so frequently weaving a web over my own heart, when — oh goodness of God, my Father! — my heart is still on a high, it is still trembling with holy joy within my breast because of how near I was to him today, because of the things he deigned to tell me, as soon as I received Communion and unexpectedly (T.638).

The weight of grace

At Communion (in spite of having been very distracted during prayer, although it was not my own fault) I felt the physical presence of Jesus more clearly than ever. It was as if the whole weight of his majesty came over me... I could hardly move inside without feeling paralyzed by my God. I felt him in my breast, not engraved there, nor only his image, but truly *embedded* in my soul.... In spite of my thoughts and other external distractions that assaulted me, this divine paralysis infinitely surpassed them, and I could not think, see or feel anything except God and only God.

This feeling did not last only during Communion, but for four hours afterwards. How can this be, Father, if the physical presence of Jesus ends quickly in Holy Communion, and I felt as if he had not left? How strange, and yet I could not doubt that he, my Jesus, was there (T.659).

Out of time

Yesterday afternoon my soul was greatly lifted up in prayer in front of the tabernacle. Even when there were a lot of people or when they were praying out loud, it was as if I did not hear or understand them, but rather felt my spirit wrapped up in God and in interior solitude with him. This is very unusual and rare for me.

Today I received my adorable Eucharist and I do not know how much time had passed, but when I came to myself I realized there was nobody left at the Communion rail. I could not remember anything, but I was sure that I had been there a long while.

My soul was on fire and, during my prayer when I thought of my sins, twice I saw my whole life, from when I was very little, pass unveiled before my very eyes. More than my sins, Father, I saw in a supernatural way all the favors and graces that God had given me, and the graces that God prepared for me in countless times of terrible danger…. I saw all of this goodness and special care… and how in spite of all my shortcomings, he has carried out his plan in the work of my spirit (T.696).

A beating heart

I had no need of faith today, I really *felt* Jesus in the tabernacle… something alive, breathing and throbbing was drawing me to that point, the center of my whole life. I would have let myself die in defense of his presence there, not only his human presence but also his divine presence, inseparable from the human, joined by the hypostatic union, inasmuch as I felt it in a very special way. I am swept away by the charms of his Most Holy Humanity, and also by the perfection, the attributes, the greatness of the Godhead of three persons, the Whole-Unity, all divine, infinite, holy.

I can feel the Most Holy Humanity of Jesus in his beauty, the door through which one can enter into the center of light and eternal fire… infinite… not made… and all of this, so sublime and incomprehensible, all this, oh God! is there, so close to us in the bread of the Eucharist! Divine love is condensed into the divine Eucharist.

Oh my adorable Eucharist, food of the soul, magnet of my existence, my life is intermingled within you! I will live as long as there is a tabernacle on this earth, yes, I will live there, even when my body returns to the dust it came from. Is this not so, Father? (T.581).

Carried to the foot of the tabernacle

I would love to live at the foot of a tabernacle! I would gladly die there... all earthly and heavenly desires leave my soul... but this is right if he is there, if I find there the full possession of all good!

Our whole being is established there, Father, within the white accidents of such a loving mystery... and we will be happy even when we are suffering the cruelest martyrdom on earth. Forgive me my good Father, but I do not know in what way I wish to force my way into and submerge myself in that little circle of the holy consecrated Host... Lord have mercy on such a bold creature! (T.856).

I could hardly pray yesterday, I am still quite ill. I prostrated myself on the floor with great effort, offering him my great poverty, and then, oh God's goodness! I had just got up when I felt myself carried to the foot of a tabernacle, feeling as never before, Father, the *live, physical and burning* presence of Jesus there, in that holy place (T.871).

Father, these last two things, feeling carried to the tabernacle and seeing, hearing and feeling these things in my soul, are very strange and new for me. I do not think they are illusions or just dreams, because I have no doubt about what happens in my soul. So what is it? Oh good Father! I am very very poor to deserve such favors... for God's sake, make me holy, Father (T.873).

God's fire

On receiving Communion, it was as if that fire and that light were growing, illuminating and warming me. For example, when coal is alight and a breeze blows over it, it comes back to life and a flame shoots up, and this is what I feel in my spirit. It is never extinguished, I mean there is always burning fuel there, but when I receive the Lord, it is set on fire, the flames shoot up, illuminating and shining.

Oh adorable Eucharist! Oh divine form, whitest Host holding heaven itself in your substance! Come, come to my arms, come to my breast, come to my soul to give it life... I can glimpse within you my beloved Trinity, my thrice holy God... that Light, that Purity, that Immensity of endless perfection! Oh come, come to me! Leave that ciborium, that tabernacle and fly to this soul that is pierced with love, dying of thirst, that loves you so very much and adores you from its poor little corner. Bring to me my beloved Father, my beloved Dove and my tender Jesus, Lily of my life, you who contain these treasures, bring them to me, quickly! because I am dying to possess them (T.1017).

The Holy Trinity

My love for the Holy Trinity has grown extraordinarily. It fills me by day and overwhelms me by night, enveloping me in mute contemplation... and absorbing me within.

I feel this most noble Trinity in the consecrated Host and in each particle, I know not how.

Hunger for my adorable Eucharist has grown. It is a voracious hunger, a hunger of the soul that cannot be compared to the hunger of the body, because the body is satisfied with anything, whereas the soul... the soul can only be satisfied with God, and only at times, because the hunger grows again, more intense than before.

I would like to receive Communion every hour, every minute, every second.... If only all my food were Communion! The nights seem eternal, and when I see the light of day my heart jumps within my breast, thinking of my other Light, Christ, my Jesus, Beauty of beauties.

If only I could take you in my unworthy hands, Oh Jesus.... How I would embrace you...! How much I would tell you, more than I can say... with your touch what might I not experience! If only I could live in the shadow of a tabernacle! I need no more heaven than this, Father. Oh my divine Sun! Jesus, Jesus, Father, my Father, beautiful Dove. How much I love them! (T.556).

My poor soul sees the beloved Trinity shine in such a way inside the white Host! Father, my Father, if only I could tell you what I feel, what I glimpse of that Holy and adorable Trinity! Even if I could explain it and repeat the same thing a thousand times, I would feel that I have said nothing and explained nothing.

I see the three Divine Persons, different from each other, but admirably joined together, inseparable, all three concurring always and eternally, none of them happier than another, none of them more perfect, none of them wiser, greater... they are eternally eternal... and perfect, and happy!

I am offended by pictures of the Father as an old man with a beard, when I see these three blessed Persons in I know not what way, all the same, all beautiful, with a beauty that is always old and always new, a beauty that the soul never tires of contemplating, feeling and adoring.... Oh God, my God! How can I explain this? I do not see a body when I am lost inside the Godhead... of course I have sometimes seen Jesus alone, with his holy body joined to his divinity (T.1018).

I was walking past a church and I felt the need to go in. I found my Jesus Eucharist exposed for adoration. As soon as I saw him my heart started beating faster, I felt the physical presence of the Lord, very clearly and without needing faith. I would

31

have staked my life on the presence there of the threefold God, my loving Trinity, my Word become flesh.

I had to drag myself away from that church where my heaven was, but my heart was very warm all day, and even though my body left the church, my spirit stayed right next to the Love of its loves (T.1021).

The tabernacle, lightning conductor of the world

I can see in the consecrated Host or the Eucharist a mystical passion, the continuation of the Lord's Passion at Calvary.... It is the same heart that suffers, and the same sins it is sacrificed for.... I can see him in a constant act of atonement, holding back divine justice, searching for souls, but holy, pure and sacrificed souls that in their union cry out to heaven for pardon and mercy.... He is tireless in this mystical crucifixion, abandoned in his solitude, infinitely patient, receiving so much ingratitude in exchange for so much love.

Oh my God, my God! What would become of the world if there were no tabernacles? They are the lightning conductors, the light, the warmth, the life... the whiteness, the purity that covers the filthy mud of the earth... Jesus is there, and almost every time I draw near him he asks me for purity, purity, crucified and clean souls to console him.... The Lord is thirsty for purity and for the Cross, and yet the world is deaf, wallowing in its dirt and sleeping on its material comforts. A terrible awakening awaits it that makes me tremble, and also makes that Heart that is all goodness to men tremble (incredible love!). He wants his Cross to reign in our hearts — only the Cross can save the world; spirits can only be sanctified through him (T.1066).

Reaching heaven

Holy joy on delighting in that ineffable and divine taste of the holy flesh of my Jesus in the Eucharist.... This effect is inexplicable, Father, and it lifts the soul from the earth and takes it to heaven. I love this consecrated Host so much, Father, that my soul would rather receive Communion than be in heaven. I accept life with all its miseries, as long as I can receive Communion in my breast, something the saints in heaven cannot do.

I see him in my soul as they see him face to face, I do not need to do that in this divine Sacrament. Oh my adorable Eucharist! you are the compendium of all the love of that divine Heart, you are my glory, my happiness, my only *life*, my heaven on earth. Being at the foot of a tabernacle is the same as being in that glory, in that heaven of endless joy. Oh come to my bosom every day of my stay on this earth! Come to give me your warmth, your strength, your virtue.... Come a thousand times, at every moment, to this bosom that loves you so much and wants to love you.

Jesus, my beloved Lord, tell me, why is the world so cold when the fiery volcano is so near? Why are souls not completely consumed along with all their iniquity? Oh my Eucharist, they do not know you, they are ignorant of what you know... and the cacophony of sin does not let them hear and count the beatings of your heart. May your purity cover them, may your immaculate whiteness enfold them (T.1069).

The center of purity

There is no stain on this precious glass (the Eucharist). Neither do I know why I understand that the greatest communication of this virtue to the soul lies in Holy Communion, and that in a *willing* heart, the holy effect of the body and blood of

Jesus Christ is amazing! What great wealth, holy God, and we do not know or appreciate it! And yet the Holy Eucharist contains the infinite depths of immaculate perfection!

I see it, I feel it, I touch it, in my understanding and in my heart. I would like to be an angel, Father, only because I think that they must be able to come closer to the clear crystal of the divine essence. But when I consider that angels do not receive Holy Communion, I am glad to be earth and dust, to which the thrice holy God comes down to purify and lift up. I feel many times in my soul the divine seed that the Lord leaves there when he passes through. What would happen to the spiritual world if it were not for the Eucharist? My soul trembles just from thinking about it! Father, may I love ever more this white consecrated Host! It is our life, our strength and that which leaves in our being the divine imprint of purity!

I can also see very clearly that Jesus communicates this virtue to the soul not from his heavenly Throne, but rather from his Eucharistic Throne, I mean from the throne of sacrifice, after being a victim on the altar, in the sacrifice of the Cross... and we are granted this grace by the price he paid with humiliation and with his blood, a grace we have to keep in humility and pain to conserve it. I do not know what union I see between purity and pain, making them inseparable, and... now it is clear! How can Jesus and the Cross ever be separated? (T.1161).

"The divine Eucharist is the infallible remedy for impurity, because it contains purity itself and my precious blood, it creates virgins and strengthens hearts by cleansing them and imbuing them with light and grace" (T.1346).

Yesterday and today my soul has felt, as it were, the aftereffects of the divinely flavored grace of my adorable Eucharist. These effects are assuring that I am on a very high level of purity, in a clear light of this heavenly virtue, and understanding very well its excellence and how much the Lord loves it. How strange, Father! It is as if I breathe in purity, and breathe out purity: purity! I long for purity, I desire purity. What can this mean? I feel a kind of respect around me, and now, every time I remember or say, "My white lily," to Jesus, my heart trembles. Oh my God, my God, blessed art thou! (T.1477).

Endlessly contemplating the Eucharist

I find unknown charms in the divine Eucharist, a bottomless depth of perfection, of love, of light, of purity! If only I could live in eternal contemplation of it! The thrice holy God is my life, my heartbeat, my everything! If only I could love him as he deserves! If I could give him the rest of my life in loving incense, burnt in sacrifice! If only I could become *all pain, all Cross, all victim* and sacrifice, even to martyrdom! I am thirsty for purity and thirsty for pain.

I feel that one thing draws another, and in my helplessness I have nothing left to give the Lord, I want to suffer, bear pain, always bear pain to console him! (T.1164).

Favors as a reward for suffering

I had a shower of suffering yesterday, as if I were the target for people and things... it was a day of many victories and humiliations.

When I received Communion today, I could feel it so big that it filled me, it filled me... it spread out... how wonderful! His physical presence was so real, I can still feel its effects.

And why? Because Jesus rewards my miseries with favors... and this brings me to my knees. It shames me and overwhelms me in his love. Some days ago, at Communion time too, the Host seemed like flowers... with a delicious and divine aroma or taste (T.1880).

35

3

JESUS' TEACHINGS ON THE EUCHARIST

Jesus' mystical passion hidden within the Eucharist

"*I am going to tell you a secret from my heart, and it is this —
my Passion has not yet finished....*"

"How can this be, Jesus?"

"*My Passion on Calvary only lasted a few hours, but the Passion of my Heart lasted all my mortal life and will last mystically in the Eucharist until the end of the world. Another secret — the Passion of my body found relief, but the Passion of my soul....*" (T.471).

Today during morning prayer Jesus told me, "*Look daughter, I let myself be seen crucified at Calvary whereas in the Eucharist I am hidden, but that does not mean I am any less present. The passion of my Heart continues still because human sin and ingratitude continue still. When I give myself to souls in this Sacrament, I find rest in so few, and so few bring me down from the Cross.... Study the hidden life in the Eucharist and in the Cross the practical life...*" (T.926).

The Eucharist makes the soul divine

I was deep in God today during prayer, but I could not enter into the prayer I had prepared for the night. I felt the physical presence of my Jesus, and then, after Communion, the precious Dove came to me and told me such wonderful and beautiful things, and the Dove will grant me light to write them down on paper.

"When you receive me, you are receiving the substance and the very Persons of the Trinity. But the three Persons make up one substance, and this substance is the Godhead, it is God. When we communicate with the soul through this Sacrament, we communicate to it this same divine substance, and this communication is so intimate that we transform the soul into our own substance if the soul is duly willing.

"This is why, you will see little daughter, the food of your dear Dove becomes the same divine substance in the milk of pure souls, and the wheat of the chosen. It is divine communication *returning to its center, God. I cannot feed on earthly things, I need my food to be* divine… *and since earth can only produce earth, that is the reason for the institution of your adorable Eucharist.*

"The soul is made divine through this Sacrament and comes nearer to its center, God. It is made one with him, like two flames that become one and cannot be separated. The world cannot penetrate the heights of this mystery of love, cannot comprehend its immense value — it contains nothing less than the most perfect union *of the soul with God.*

"You see, the Holy Trinity, of which I am the Third Person, cannot be separated from its image, because it is its own very highly esteemed image. Where the beautiful Trinity is reflected, it is not reflected but present. And so the soul that reflects or portrays it, this soul possesses the Holy Trinity real and present, not as a reflection or a portrait. There are however, different levels. The purer the light in which it is seen reflected, the greater the communication of its ef-

fect and beauty. Sometimes it can be felt, as you have experienced; at other times it is hidden to the soul, but it imparts the same degrees of grace and love.

"The secret of communication and union *is present in what I say to you. It is a free gift, because God is master of what is his own and can give it to whomever he pleases, even if it is not deserved.*

"You see — the Father's substance is love, and it is such a great love for mankind that he gave his own Son to redeem the world.

"The Son's substance is love, and it is such a great love for the Father and for mankind that he gave himself over to pain to save mankind and to honor the Father. My own substance, that of the Third Person, is love, love for the glory of the Trinity, the same as the Father and the Son, taking part in the mystery of the Incarnation, continuing in the life of Jesus, bearing witness to his divinity, sealing the Work of Redemption, giving shelter to the Church, my immaculate Wife.

"The substance of the Father is Love and Power. My substance is Love and Life, the substance of the Son is Love and Pain. The substance of the three Persons of the Trinity is Charity, the purest love of communication. It is called Charity because it communicates and is the most perfect Love of Charity.

"Pain, or the Cross made divine by the Son, is the only step to ascend to love. Do you understand the value of the Cross now? This is why you will see that the genuinely crucified are those who love most, because pain, Jesus' banner, draws the three Divine Persons behind it. We live in that soul and I make my nest in it" (T.520).

He also told me, *"You see, my daughter, God takes pleasure in himself and in the souls that are transformed* into him *(whenever they can), because he sees there his own divine image. There is no better way of being transformed into him than taking part in the Holy Eucharist in Communion, but not only in the union of the divine substance (I mean in thoughts, because this is not really possible), but rather the human substance crucified as a victim... like me.*

39

"*The soul that understands all this and receives the Host as the God-Host, as the Divine-Human-Victim, such as this Eucharistic Sacrament is in reality, this happy soul cannot but burn, transforming itself into the two fires that consume the Holy Eucharist, the fire of love and mystically in the fire of pain.*"

Jesus desires the imitation of his sacrifice in the Holy Eucharist, by his living Crosses, the Sisters of the Cross. I can feel within me a vast field regarding this that I cannot explain (T.594).

The purifying effect of the Eucharist

"*My daughter, I wish to possess you, I want to* absorb you *in myself, in the immensity of my pain and in my infinite joy. I want union, union, an intimate union, that I have been asking you for a long time, and yet I who am Purity itself, I join myself to whatever is pure… I who am Holiness itself, I join myself to whatever is holy, and I who am Divinity itself, I only join myself to what has been made divine….*"

"But Jesus," I said, "how can you want to be joined to me, I who am neither pure, nor holy, nor made divine, but rather very material. What can I do, Jesus, to bring this about?"

"*The Eucharist makes man divine, it purifies him and makes him holy. He will always find everything he needs in the Eucharist, since it is the Nest of all that is holy, pure and divine. You, my daughter, have not been purified as much as I need you to be. You need me, and you need to be made* one substance with the Cross. *You have to lose yourself in it, be one with it, so that you can be united with your Jesus.*

"*You see, my daughter, the eucharistic rays are the ones that purify and unite the fastest, but they only go through souls that have been turned into the Cross*" (T.558).

The mystery of the heart of Jesus

On the 18th at morning prayer, the Lord made me understand something about the mysteries of his divine heart, that is about his love in the Holy Eucharist and on the Cross....

My heart was filled with gratitude and admiration on seeing how these two things are related and almost condensed into just one, seeing the Cross in the Eucharist and the Eucharist in the Cross.... Light was shed on this for me and yet since I did not write it down, maybe the Lord was unhappy with me and did not give me anything in my other prayers, nor let me coordinate my ideas, leaving me dry.

And then Jesus said to me, *"You see, daughter, I gave myself to you in the Eucharist before I did so on the Cross. I was crucified first in the Eucharist, giving myself to mankind in a profound immolation, before mankind crucified me on the material Cross. Sacrifice comes before love when it is true, and I was already alive on the Cross for you throughout my whole life, before I was crucified externally in the eyes of all men. I was willingly nailed to the Eucharist before the material Cross, binding myself there with the greatest love....*

"The Eucharist is your Jesus, but your Jesus on the Cross, because the Eucharist is my mystical Cross where I separate my body and my blood as I did on Calvary, always for the salvation of an ungrateful mankind. I have been crucified for centuries for man in the Eucharist, and yet I was only materially crucified for him for a few hours. My Passion has not yet finished, because sin has not yet come to an end, and for as long as there is sin in man there will be sacrifice in Jesus.

"Sacrifice yourself with me to console me, I am thirsty for sacrifice.... This world only gives me bitterness in its sensuality — so few remember that I am here in the tabernacle the same as on the Cross, praying and offering myself for them to the Eternal Father! Do not forget me... think of me..." (T.928).

41

The union of two natures in the Eucharist

"In the Sacrament of the altar I left my BODY and my BLOOD, but it is clear that this body and blood were not dead, but that I was alive in order to be sacrificed. *And my body has a soul.*

"The ceremony of the body and the blood is carried out on the altar in order that there might be a sacrifice, so that the sacrifice may exist, but I am in the bread and in the wine together and separately, and wholly even in just one portion of these consecrated items.

"I, in the Eucharist, being SEPARATE I would say (what the Lord means is that it is not exactly the Trinity that is worshiped in the Eucharist), *I am not me. Since the Incarnation of the Word I have been so joined to the Godhead that I cannot be separated from it even for a moment. It is a* special *union, turning man into God and God into man, but the man is not really God because he cannot stop being a man, and neither is God totally a man because he cannot stop being God. He is both God and man, the Word made flesh. He did not stop being God just because he took on human nature, neither did he abandon his will, his power, his actions or attributes. The Incarnation of the Word brought about the union of two natures, of two wills, a transformation of man into God, who while he did not stop being man, is* the true, real, passive and living God. *And yet these two natures and wills made up* just one *Divine Person, with two essences — divine and human — and two substances – human and divine."*

"But tell me, my Jesus. Is the Word within your Holy Humanity, or is the Humanity within the Word?"

"The Word became flesh, daughter, not the flesh Word… but the Word is in the flesh, not filling my body with a Divine Person, since this is evident. Jesus' soul was in his body, but the Word was in both his soul and his body in a special union, UNIQUE and real.

"My Holy Humanity alone, no matter how holy, pure and perfect it might have been, could not have done anything. Every miracle I worked, every doctrine I taught and all the holy things I

42

did, I received all of them from the Word, from the Divine Person that was in me" (T.1922).

I knew from when I was very young that Jesus wanted to speak.

"You see, the Eucharist, where I am, is a mystery of unity. It participates, if we can say it like this, more than any other mystery, in unity. And why? Because it is a mystery of love, of a unique love, of a most intense, divine and human love.

"It is true that in the Eucharist my body is present and loved, but since the Godhead is united to my body and to my soul, the Godhead in me is adored, the divine substance in me is adored, and my holy body is also adored.

"My body and my soul are created in this substance, but the Godhead was not created, although it is in me giving me heavenly vitality, produced by the divine substance of God himself".

"Lord, tell me, what is this *substance*, what does it consist of?"

"It is what feeds bodies and sanctified souls with the divine. I am not converted into substance, it is the substance of the bread and the wine that is converted into me, and this is the miracle and the mystery for mankind — I am not only in the Host by the divine power in me, but in the substance or particles of each wafer, in each drop of consecrated wine of all chalices, in thousands of Hosts and chalices at the same time.

"But do you know why I am not divided? Because I am one, indivisible, and even though I am multiplied I do not lose my unity.

"Because I live in the Father, as both God and man, and the Father is in me. The miracle of transubstantiation takes place like an all-powerful miracle communicated to my Humanity, with the power of the Divine Word, God with the Father and the Holy Spirit within me, with the infinite power of unity.

"Unity, C.,[9] *is love, and love is unity. Do you not remember*

---

[9] Sic. in the original Spanish. It stands for the author's name, Conchita (translator's note).

when I said that he who knows me knows my Father? Was I refer-
ring to my body? My Father has no body, I was referring to my di-
vinity, to the Word within me, exactly the same as the Father, be-
cause the Trinity only has one aspect, the Godhead, *in which all*
the beauty and loveliness that were not created are contained, ev-
erything that heaven and earth should adore and love in ecstasy"
(T. 3496).

The Eucharist and the Cross

Later, Father, as if in a great fire Jesus spoke to me and said,
"The school of saints is to be found in the Cross and in the Eucha-
rist. This is where the soul is taught, where it learns... where we
suffer, where we love... this is where the soul retreats to from the
earth... where it draws near to heaven... here it is tested and re-
warded... here it is purified and sanctified... here it dies to come
back to life and live....

"You see, daughter, the Eucharist and the Cross, Love and
Pain, are so united that nothing can separate them. I am crucified
here at all times, mystically, and the blood of Calvary is the blood
on the altar, and the body offered as a victim on the Cross is the
wafer of the eucharistic sacrifice.

"Love and suffer, daughter, suffer and love. Do not stray from
the Cross or from the Eucharist. Bear souls, especially the one I have
entrusted to you for its perfection. Teach the wealth of pain, of pa-
tient sacrifice, of voluntary crucifixion, of living sacrifice, that is, the
treasures of the Cross. But teach as well where to find the source of
strength, infinite love, the greatest manifestation of a God's tender-
ness, the Eucharist. Divine substance conquers human nature. May
souls love me, my daughter. I want love, but a love of purity and
sacrifice."

This lit my soul up and I did not want to leave my beloved
tabernacle (T.1507).

The Consecration

"How is it that you are said, Jesus, to come down to the priest's hands in the Consecration, as if from heaven — how can this be if you are so close?"

"I am everywhere," he answered, *"and I am sacrificed on thousands of altars at the same time.... My coming down means that the words pronounced by the priest turn the bread into my flesh and the wine into my blood. All of me passes into these sacramental substances, and my Calvary is renewed, my death on the Cross, the purest atonement and sacrifice... and the priests are distracted... and many offend me... and how often the faithful do not think that I am converted into a victim for them in the priest's hands!"*

And I felt, Father Felix, that I would then hear Mass with greater fervor, and when I told you and you told the Oasis, they would do the same.... Oh Father! those hands that touch purity itself, that are stained with the divine blood of a voluntary and most holy victim... they should be so pure! Those lips that have the power, Oh God! to bring Jesus to the altar of sacrifice... what should they be like! Should they not be like crystal that nothing can ever cloud?

And the body, the heart and the soul that receives him, Oh Father of my soul! how white, how spotless, how innocent they should be to receive the white Lily, the divine Lily, stained with the blood of love! I do not know how many things I understood... felt... about priests, what they should be like! I have another doubt, my dear Jesus.

"Tell me, what do you mean when you say to me that you are sacrificed for every soul that receives you in Holy Communion, living once more your sacrifice and death on Calvary to give purity and life. And yet I see that the priest with the same words consecrates any number of Hosts, one or a thousand, how can this be? Would you not need a sacrifice for each one?"

"My sacrifice is vast and the virtue contained in the words of

the Consecration has power not only for me to pass into the substance, or for them to become me in one wafer. For it is the same, with nothing lost, for me to be in thousands, as it is for me to be in the smallest particle, in the chalice and in the Host, and even though the Host and the wine are separate, so that the sacrifice separates my body and my blood, I am present in both things" (T.1736).

"*The words of the Consecration are words of CREATION, BOTH AFFIRMATIVE AND IMPERATIVE, that is the seal of God, the seal of the Godhead, of the eternal Word, the one who wished to leave my LOVE to my Church as a legacy.*

"*They are words of CREATION because in one instant they convert the Sacramental substance into my very body and my very blood by their POWER. In a way, they give me my being, like a new Incarnation.*"

"But if you spill all your blood in each Mass, how can this be, Jesus? What is left for the other thousand?"

"*The same blood is left, NOT ANOTHER DIFFERENT, either created or renewed, the same blood that I received from Mary and the same blood as on Calvary. It already existed in the divine understanding, rescuing mankind from sin and from hell.*

"*This is my power of the words of CREATION in the Consecration, a special and omnipotent power, that creates not only another body and another blood, but MY body and MY blood. This takes place thousands of times, and neither the words of power nor the victim are changed — I am always me. They are AFFIRMATIVE words, because they are pronounced by God, not by man. It is true that they come from the lips of a man, but made divine as it were, and in those sublime moments they come from the Godhead itself, with all its power and Truth.*

"*God is Truth, and the eternal Truth, and there cannot be even the shadow of a deception in him. Whatever he says, whatever he affirms, is true. Even the smallest doubt would be a sin against the faith, against God himself. God is the eternal word, and whatever proceeds from him should be BELIEVED and ADORED, with all the strength of one's mind and heart.*

"They are IMPERATIVE words. In the words of the Conse-cration, the Man-God orders and demands. He does not beg, he does not give freedom of choice. 'He who wants to follow me,' 'He who wants to be my disciple,' etc., but rather with all the power of the Godhead he joined the command to creative action, and orders man to eat that victim and to drink all his blood. Not a piece of the victim and some of the blood but the whole and entire thing, which is found in any sacramental substance. And this atoning, divine and human victim is found in every Mass. He orders this thousands of times, constantly, in the holy words of the Consecration.

"And why does God order people to 'eat my flesh' and 'drink my blood,' daughter; why rather do I, God and man, order this?

"The aim is always love, because I could not order in any other way, I would not be able to.

"In my infinite gentleness I order mankind to be happy.... I order him to EAT me, because I am consumed by the burning desire to be near him, joined to him to make him happy.

"I want him to share in my divine and human perfection, to make him holy, and this makes me beside myself as it were, because the Man-God's infinite love for mankind is stupendous, my daughter! And is this great favor appreciated and esteemed, not only by the faithful, but also, daughter, by my priests who have been granted this power of creation, the power of God himself to work for themselves and for others the most amazing and infinite act of Charity?

"Souls who have been listening for centuries and centuries, souls who eat this body and drink this blood, they are so few! If they only knew what they stood to gain by receiving me, not only through love but also because of the benefits of union with me, the whole world would receive Communion every day. One of the greatest torments of eternity, daughter, is not have made the most of this eucharistic treasure.

"This is another painful secret of my heart — that human ingratitude should scorn the omnipotence of creation, the truth of affirmation, even the commanding order of love in its essence" (T.1931).

Why did Jesus establish the Eucharist?

He started to tell me the following, and I was hanging on his every word, listening and loving, writing this down:

"I was humbled in the Incarnation, and this is the first and greatest step from all eternity that will never take place again. After so many other steps, daughter, this is the last one and it will last till the end of time; it is the Eucharist.

"Mankind needed to see me and touch me —— matter always needs matter. What a great humbling! Infinitely greater than the first time, not only because of the contact with sin, as in the Incarnation (on taking on human nature), but because of the contact with both the sinner and the sin... but LOVE always discovers the ways of love, *ways of* the same substance, *and my love found a way, related to the substance of which this love is made in dealing with mankind,* the substance of humility, *and I remain on the altar till the end of time.*

"But what is the main reason for this? The end objective is always Charity, immense love, *to make souls and men's bodies eternally happy, feeding them with my own body and soul, transforming them with my substance of the Godhead, making them divine....*

"I am joined, I am identified not only with the soul that calls me with the divine seal inside it, but also with the body that sometimes resists my entering into it. And how many times it does not allow me to communicate purity, holiness, assimilation in the sacrifice and PAIN! through contact with me, but a pain wrapped in tenderness and love!

"This is the main reason, daughter, why the WORD became flesh... to be flesh from flesh, after feeling not its sin, because my flesh was sinless, but rather its pain, its needs, its very POVERTY! God's sovereign love deigned to do this!" (T.1918).

"Tell me, Jesus. If the redemption was enough for your justice to wash away sin, if this bridged the distance that existed between God and man, as you told me, between heaven and earth, so tell me, why do you perpetuate the same sacrifice of the Cross on your altar? Why did you remain with man, my God, to be scorned?"

"*Only for LOVE, my daughter, only for love. But there are many other reasons derived from this one. I remain on the altar because of a sublime thirst, daughter, that consumes the Word made flesh, taking joy in the sacrifice I made for mankind....*

"*I stayed to complete souls with my life as a victim on the altar, the sacrifice they still need... I stayed to keep on atoning for man's ingratitude, WITH BLOOD, daughter, with A PERPETUAL SACRIFICE....*

"*I stayed in order to be* the only pure victim, *reminding the offended Godhead of my sacrifice on the Cross and pouring forth graces for souls, laying aside their just sentence. All sacrifice would be useless without me, daughter, and so by perpetuating my sacrifice, forgiveness is also perpetuated, and mankind's sacrifice acquires worth through union with me.*

"*I stayed in order to draw souls by example to love PAIN in all its forms. I stayed, my daughter, for the* pleasure *given to the Word made flesh in being near his creatures, heart to heart...what goodness!*

"*I stayed, as I have told you, in order to live closer, in continuous contact with mankind, and to annul his ingratitude with my abasement, with my tenderness and love!*

"*You see, my daughter, the unheard-of abjection of the Word in the Incarnation has brought incalculable good to mankind, and man is not even grateful! Among these good things is the fact that I, your Jesus, took on FLESH and the attributes of mankind, the desire for* love, communication and closeness *to other people, whose substance I possess.*

"*All this kept me here, daughter, and* even though I went back *to the Father, to glorify the flesh I had taken in Mary's virgin bosom,* I also stayed, *because of the secret of* union, attraction and communication *that all flesh bears within. The only difference is*

49

that in me all this is most holy and its aim is always to make those around me happy.

"And as I have said to you, man is material and needs material things, he needs to feel in his senses what he loves. This is part of his being. As I knew this NEED, and I was also THIRSTY FOR HIS LOVE, that is why I took on the most humble, the most common, the most ordinary, the daily food of both the rich and the poor, a piece of bread, a little piece of bread, as I said, humbling not only for a God, but even for a slave. After the INCARNATION I stayed on the altar in the form of the Sacrament…

"I am happy, daughter, with the transubstantiation of the bread and wine…. I desire to be sacrificed at all times, daughter, and my heart is impatient for this to take place when I am on the altar…. I ardently and vehemently desire, as you have seen (Oh my God!), to be sacrificed for mankind and on his behalf! Oh incomprehensible mysteries of God's LOVE! Man sinned by crucifying me and I wash away his crime each time that the same man crucifies me on the altar."

"But why, my God? I am horrified by this!"

"Because the priest is not a sinner there, he represents me, the pure and immaculate Lamb, who takes away the sins of the world. He represents me, who was sacrificed first in the cenacle. Again, it is not really a man who sacrifices me, it is the priest transformed into a Man-God, into the Word itself made flesh, who offers me to the Godhead, to the Trinity, and offers himself too as an atoning victim in union with me to repair and to save. The priest is at the same time the one who sacrifices and the victim.

"How great, how sublime and how holy is the priest's ministry! He should be more like me than anybody else in everything he does! I suffer everything in the eucharistic Sacrament, because it is the MYSTERY OF LOVE and not harshness… in which I forgive… atone…. I am a constant VICTIM, filling THE NEED to make souls happy WITH THIS DIVINE THIRST.

"Since God is God, my daughter, there can be no need in him. He is altogether content in himself, but your Word… your

Word made flesh, WISHED TO EXPERIENCE NEED, the same needs as mortal man, along with his pains, in order to sanctify them, and his feelings in order to purify them. This is why THE WORD BECAME FLESH.

"*However, my life on earth was drawing to an end and I could not fill my thirst for pain... for poverty... for humility... for obedience... for patience... for sacrifice and self-denial, and for many other virtues. This is why even my Heart became sad. Oh incomparable love! And yet divine omnipotence came to help mankind (mankind's feelings), and thought up and carried out a way of filling his need for love. By establishing the Eucharist, I voluntarily entered into it, and am captive there until the end of time. I do not suffer as in my earthly life, but in my eucharistic life I suffer mystically, in happiness, daughter, with just one soul to keep me company.*

"*Do you now have an idea about the love of a God, of the Word, of your Jesus, of that trinity, the Word, Jesus and his soul, absorbed in the Trinity itself? And your Word, just as at the Incarnation, knew that he would be scoffed at, hated and scorned in the Eucharist, by man. But did that stop him? No! because for the love of God there are no barriers that cannot be overcome. And he will live in his Church till the end of time and on the altar,* available not only for the holy man, as could well happen (having demanded it thus), but also for the ungrateful and vile man who tramples on him, for the impure and sacrilegious sinner!

"*You cannot understand the ultimate martyrdom of your Jesus-Eucharist when he enters into stained hearts*" (T.1921).

"*The mystery of the Eucharist contains many mysteries, many loves, humility and pain.*

"*With my body and my blood I want to remind man of the Passion of the Man-God, in order to rescue and save him.*

"*I want to remind him of the love of the Man for man, of the secrets of that immense love, that in union with the Godhead humbled itself and suffered to save man from sin and help him attain to heaven.*

"*How great are the aims of Charity in the Eucharist!*" (T.1922).

How sublime is the priestly ministry!

"But when I enter into sacrilegious souls, oh daughter! the Word cannot atone because of the intimate contact not only with sin, but with the SINNER. It can only PUNISH.

"That is why the worst torture for me is to enter into a sacrilegious soul with my divinity.

"I took on sin at the Incarnation, but in Communion it is as if sin took on me, and instead of being able to atone, since I am God and precisely because I am God, I have to punish. And for me, daughter, punishing is the MOST PAINFUL thing that exists, because it is contrary to my nature of love.

"However, all of God's attributes glorify him, and being forced to justice, he does not stop being content" (T.1921).

The world is fed by the Eucharist

"Take note of these words, of the secrets of their love, for there are many. It was this love that wished to work the incredible and amazing miracle of transubstantiation, conceiving me in each consecrated Host, feeding the world not only with my divine memory, but with my life, all of me, enriching the Church with my physical presence in the tabernacle and enriching souls with all the treasures of heaven" (T.2839).

Souls that continue the Passion of Jesus

"Another secret — I am the Body and soul of the Church, and all my people are part of this Body and in union with me they should continue atonement and sacrifice till the end of time. This is not understood and much less put into practice, which is why in these days I have come in search of victims, in the Oasis, to fill this vast void with my redemptive goals. That is the reason for the Catena,

daughter, to continue making atonement for an ungrateful and corrupt world. That is why I demand purity and sacrifice, to fulfil the loving aims of your Word, who constantly humbles and sacrifices himself on the altar, voluntarily" (T.1916).

I had been there for half an hour when the Lord thought fit to say what follows.

"*My daughter, why did I say 'Take this and eat, this is my body; take and drink for this is my blood,' if not to transform the creature into me? What else could I want from the Sacrament except this unification, making man divine not only through contact with me but also with my divine substance to make him one with me? I do not intend this Sacrament to be just an assimilation, but rather a transubstantiation into me, a transformation by means of compenetration, union, rather unity, a poor creature absorbs divine power turning him into God.*

"*This is why the Sacrament of the altar is the Sacrament of love par excellence. But it first required the Incarnation to communicate the divinity of the Word to human flesh, ennobling it, purifying it and making it worthy by this compenetration of immortality in the resurrection.*

"*Is it therefore strange that I should wish and ask souls that are joined to me to say to the Father, 'This is my body, this is my blood,' with the condition, of course, that their body and blood are pure or purified from all stain, victims of the same sacrifice as mine, with the same loving aims.*

"*If only the Church and Christians would really form one body with mine, one blood with mine, I mean one* sole *heart and sacrifice with me as the Head! The world would change beyond recognition and the Father would be greatly glorified!*

"*Then this nucleus of souls would continue my Passion on earth and cry out to heaven in union with me as pure Hosts. 'This is my body, this is my blood, this is us with him and him with us and in us. We ask you, beloved Father, for the salvation of the world, the triumph of the Church, the reign of the Holy Spirit, peace, etc.'*

"*With this unified cry of those who are mine, with this incense of propitiation, with this Treasure of atonement and entreaty, my heavenly Father will be appeased and the earth will be renewed.*

"And when I said 'Do this in memory of me,' of course I was not speaking only to priests. It is true that only they have the power to change the substance of the bread into my holy body and the substance of the wine into my blood by the words of the Consecration. But the joining of all sacrifices into one is a matter for all Christians. Resembling the victim of the altar through faith and through the victim's works, offering me to the eternal Father as a lightning conductor for divine justice, as a Host of propitiation, this is something all Christians have to do, as members of one body.

"Today I tell you, 'Do this in memory of me. Offer me and offer yourself in union with all your people, and this will purify you. This will enkindle you with love. It will unite you ever more closely to the Word. It will cause you to partake of a painful but divine joy. And all martyrdom will seem gentle compared to this act that encompasses a loving mandate from uncreated Love.

"You are a host, but you have to be pure and self-sacrificing. You are a host, not alone but with me in your heart, me crucified. You are a living Cross, which means you are a host, holding in its arms the Redeemer and Savior who wants to pour forth his grace, but who cannot find enough victim souls in a voluntary sacrifice with him to offer themselves to the eternal Father on behalf of the world.

"Many sins have been committed by priests and need to be atoned for, my daughter, many crimes that wound my sensitive heart. Come, make haste, do not be afraid of pain for I am with you. Sacrifice yourself and sacrifice me, lift me up on high and even though your body and soul are broken in pieces, even though you feel yourself being crushed, in peace and in joy within your pain say, 'This is my body, this is my blood.' Even though you are poor and wretched, by your transformation into me you will obtain grace, and this grace will be fruitful because of my infinite merits.

"This is what the Holy Spirit wants, voluntary victims to pour themselves out, united to the Word he loves so much. This is what the Father wants, and this is what I invite you to in order to please

them. May all your people join together and cry out in one voice to heaven, offering themselves and offering me. Have mercy!"

"Lord, are there not other souls who can do this? There are so many good souls for you to take pleasure in. You can see that I am not good enough".

"Yes, there are those who can, and especially religious souls (not taking words but rather substance), but I am speaking to you and to those I have given you, since it is a question of having a special predilection for the Work."

The Lord has inspired me so much that I cannot stop myself and I am offering him as he wishes, feeling unspeakable pleasure in my soul. Why have I overlooked the Lord's graces for so long? (T.2850).

The Eucharist, a fountain of fertility and of virginity

The Lord told me today something that made me pray in silence, a very profound silence in which the soul seems to be asleep, and yet it is far from it, in a state of great activity — LOVING, and only loving! And how can I avoid these effects?

"Lose yourself, daughter, in the preexistent Godhead that has loved you for all eternity, receive its reflections, its beauty and give them back to your Word in humble love....

"This is how your Word loved you, and this is how you and all your children should love him. Lose yourself in me by working always towards love. If you possess me and I possess you, how can you help being all Charity?"

And my soul was bathed in silent contemplation. I thought he had finished talking but suddenly he said, *"Do you remember the substance that I explained at length to you, telling you that the substance in God is life? Well, you see, this can be applied to the Eucharist. I am in the substance of the bread and wine. What you see in the Host and in the wine is like the wrapping of the substance that turns into me.*

"The substance is food, like the essence of food, which is why the substance of the bread and wine becomes my own Substance from which all substances proceed, to be FOOD, daughter, food for the body and for the soul, even of those who crucify me. Could there be greater love than this?

"Transubstantiation consists of changing the substance of the bread and wine into my own Substance. I do not change my Substance into the substance of the bread. It is the bread that, by virtue of the sacred words, becomes my own Substance, which is one and eternal, and cannot be changed.

"This is why when the bread and wine turn into my own Substance, they are transformed into one thing alone, God in three Divine Persons (I am speaking of the divinity of the Word, one with the Father and the Holy Spirit), not three substances but one Substance and one Essence in the transubstantiation: MY BODY AND MY BLOOD, and with them the Word, and with the Word the other Divine Persons that cannot be separated from the beautiful unity that they have.

"Listen to another secret. The Eucharist is a virgin because I am a virgin, and the virginity of Mary is reflected and impressed on my soul. Mary's virginity was nothing more than a reflection of the Trinity, although a very intense reflection, eternally a virgin, because the only intercourse she had was divine, holy, spiritual and at the same time most fruitful.

"All virginity proceeds from the virginity of the Trinity, and this virginity shines especially bright in the Eucharist and in its effect upon the soul.

"That is why I do not allow yeast in the Host whose substance is to be turned into me, since I do not allow impulsive intercourse because of my virginity, and that is why I also demand purity of the souls that are to receive me."

"And what about the body, my Jesus?"

"When the soul is clean, pure or purified, the body is clean too."

"But tell me, Lord. If you love virginity so much, why did you establish marriage?"

"Marriage is holy, daughter, and its fruitfulness is a reflection of God's fruitfulness, to propagate mankind. But I have already explained to you at length how the soul can remain virgin even within marriage.

"It is mankind who twists the pure and the holy, but everything that proceeds from the hands of God is perfect. Also, people are free to marry or to remain single."

"Oh my God! Why did you not let me embrace virginity? You love it so much!"

"Because of my lofty aims, so that my glory would shine brighter" (T.1922).

"My Father did not only eternally beget me, the Divine Word, but he also perpetuates that fruitfulness in his virgin bosom. And in order to take greater pleasure in the reflection, or rather in the reality of that moment without beginning, he perpetuates this holy fruitfulness in the Mass, multiplying me in the Sacrament while being one, and bringing about a transubstantiation with infinite fruitfulness" (T.3291).

4

THE EUCHARIST, MARY AND PRIESTS

Mary, the nest of the Eucharist

Jesus also says that the beloved Eucharist has a nest. Oh Father, what a beautiful nest! He says that this nest is the pure Heart of Mary, and all pure hearts. Let us be the Eucharist's nest, Father, its warmth, its *rest*.... I feel like throwing myself into the divine fire, and I would love to see it burn and be consumed for the Beloved!

If only I could die as the pure nest of the one who is all purity and whiteness, the adorable and pure Host... holy... immaculate... Jesus Eucharist!

The Eucharist, the body of Christ from Mary, under attack by Satan

"Let me tell you another secret. Since that blessed flesh proceeds from Mary, it is the enemy of Satan, having the same substance as Mary.[10] *That is why Satan hates the Eucharist, because of Mary's*

---

[10] Let us make this clear. A person who receives Communion only receives in the Sacrament the Body of Christ, not the body of Mary. However, the eucharistic body is intimately related to the Mother of God since it is related to the body that was born of Mary in the Incarnation.

participation in the Word incarnate. It is his worst torment.

"And let me tell you yet another secret. Satan deeply hates the souls I choose for the mystical Incarnation, an imitation of the Incarnation in Mary, but he cannot get near them. His limits are clearly marked, and this makes him desperate.

"Anything that reflects the Incarnation consumes him... and as for the Eucharist, what greater reflection could there be, daughter, to exasperate him? The Eucharist is a perpetual Incarnation in the soul, another kind of Incarnation that ends when the Sacrament ends, leaving behind only its effects, but it is still an Incarnation. This is why Satan fights it so cruelly, because he knows the good it does to the soul, which does not give me anything and yet receives an abundance of grace and worth.

"And do you know what is, among many others, the purpose of the Eucharist? It is the glorification of bodies for the resurrection.

"Nobody can go to heaven unless he participates of my substance and is assimilated to my very Being. And the Eucharist, daughter, is the most powerful means for achieving this transformation — it leaves the seed of immortality for eternal glorification in the soul and body that receives it with the right attitude" (T.1918).

The Eucharist, Mary and priests

"There is no other favor for mankind like the Eucharist — it is the most powerful means for the intimacy and union of the soul with its God. And this mystery of sublime and perpetual love is to be found in my Church.

"Priests in a way fulfil the role of the Holy Spirit in the Incarnation, and Mary is represented by my Church — pure, immaculate and holy just like her! The Church is the reflection of Mary; it is her daughter and like her, fruitful in its virginity.

"All souls that receive me in the Eucharist, daughter, should be fruitful in their virginity like this! Fruitful in purity and in all virtues! My flesh and my blood are pure and fruitful in grace and

worth — this is why the one who receives me receives supernatural life that detaches him from the earth and brings him near to heaven" (T.1920).

Mary's blood

"I took my blood in Mary, and so if they are my blood, they must proceed from her; they must have obtained their lifeblood and all the seeds of holiness that go with it from the Immaculate Virgin.

"I can faithfully say that Mary was my blood and so the most intimately related person to me, more than anybody else, and the one who most cooperated in union with me for the salvation of the world through the union of her love and pain which was one with mine" (T.2430).

Mary, the Eucharist and the Holy Spirit

"And look how the Holy Spirit had a part in the fruitfulness of these words in the Consecration. The Holy Spirit plays a very important role in the Eucharist, which is hardly ever, if at all, taken into account. He reflects the Incarnation once again, and in a way reproduces it through the holy words and in each soul that receives Communion" (T.2919).

Priests should call on Mary in order to participate in the Eucharist

Later on he told me, *"This is why Mary has such a great and intimate role in the Mass, and all priests should call on her to accompany them when saying Mass.*

"If only priests would do this, they would be converted in such numbers! The Immaculate Virgin would remind them of their duty

to be angels! The Throne of Wisdom would always remind them of the Divine Word, the Word that should inspire them with knowledge and virtue!

"The Church would gain so much if its priests studied, imitated and loved Mary in their eucharistic relations and in the martyrdoms that they were worthy of!

"May missionaries be models, may they draw near the altar reflecting Mary, pronouncing the words of the Consecration worthily" (T.2921).

"It is true that when I pronounced these words of creation, I thought of Mary, from whose body I took my own body, and from whose blood I took my own blood. She could honestly say to the soul in reference to the Eucharist, 'This is my body, this is my blood' (in me), because it was really and literally a body from her body and blood from her blood. Nobody else could say this in truth and without sin" (T.2922).

Is Mary present in the Eucharist?

I said, "Lord, is Mary physically present at Mass?"

"Her soul is there, her presence, her tender love, for she does not leave her Son. I alone, though, am present on the altar body and soul, as God and as Man."

"But is Mary not in heaven with her body as well?"

"Yes, her soul and her immaculate body are there, but during Mass only I come down at the priest's words of creation that bring about transubstantiation, and I will also come down in my glorious and physical body at the final judgment."

"But Lord, Mary has also come down to earth in her virgin body in Tepeyac and in Lourdes, etc."

"Yes, but these outward graces for the world are rare, not frequent, and their holy and vast goals are always for my glory."

"But why does Mary not come down in her body in Mass?

This would be beautiful, and her glorified body would not take up space."

"It is not a question of taking up material space, but rather that my Wisdom has thus decreed it. Her living presence is there in Mass, her mother's heart adoring the Divine Son together with the priest.

"And yet Mary's maternal heart also shudders and weeps together with the unworthy priest, and it suffers mystically, not so much at the vile and treacherous offense I suffered as Man and as God, but rather at the unheard-of offense that my Father suffered, and at the punishment that the unfaithful priest deserves, since we have one heart and one heartbeat" (T.3406).

A priest's responsibility towards the Eucharist

Woe to the world without this pure, holy and immaculate victim, constantly sacrificed on the altar for its atonement and purification!

Woe to the souls that do not have Jesus Christ in the tabernacle! Poor me! if I do not have that consecrated Host that is my life, my strength, my only love and desire, my only joy and happiness. If I could only give my blood right down to the last drop for the beloved Church, for the doctrine that is scorned, for so much grace that is wasted and trampled on. Jesus, Jesus! Your ministers are sometimes the first to more or less see this liquid treasure spilled out from your very heart!

Oh my God, let me weep for this great misfortune with tears from my soul! They treat you, Lord, and your divine Sacraments with such a lack of respect, with such impure hearts and hands! How can you allow this to happen, Lord, how can you suffer it in such profound silence? Faith, Lord, faith! Shed your divine light on those minds that have been darkened by... shall I say it? (a hidden force makes me say it clearly!), darkened by vice… and you suffer, Lord, in the silence of the tabernacle you weep at the insults, at the loss of those poor souls.

Mercy, Lord, have mercy! I can see, Father, although I do not know how, the terrible judgment awaiting those priests who neither receive nor give the precious blood of Jesus Christ as they should… who do not work at their own holiness, in order to fruitfully sow the divine seed in hearts. The priests who live in the Church of the Lord like parasites have an enormous responsibility… I can feel the profound complaints of the divine Heart about this, something that deeply deeply hurts him!

If only with my blood and with my life, with my crucifixion, I could alleviate the pain of this divine Heart so maltreated by his own! My soul is in pain, Father, and I wish to be a victim. I want to suffer, and belonging entirely to God, I want to sacrifice myself for the holy and pure Church, where he has put his heavenly riches (T.1170).

Pure priests

"I need worthy and pure priests as victims, I mean, just as you saw me, pure white and constantly yearning for the sacrifice. I would gladly join them to myself in the sacrifice on the altar, offering both of us at the same time for the salvation of the world" (T.1736).

Jesus humiliated by unworthy priests

"Yes, daughter, you should know this. I am constantly entering into impure souls, a terrible crime that will be punished by my justice with the worst torture! This is a fairly constant thing too in my priests, who should be pure, chosen and clean vessels not only to receive me but to keep me in them consoling me and giving me to console with sacrifices of love" (T.1920).

The greatness and mystery of the priesthood

"The priest brings about on the altar, daughter, an exact copy of the Incarnation of the Word. It is as if, with the words of the Consecration, he creates, that is, gives life (this is the divine virtue inherent in those words) to a Being, a Being that is both divine and human, called God and man, the Word made flesh, your Jesus. The priest does not and cannot give life to God, because God IS LIFE. *He does not and cannot give life to the God-Man, because He lives and will live eternally glorified. Rather he transmits that divine and human life into the substance of the bread and the substance of the wine, bringing about the* transubstantiation *by the power of his words, so that what was before just bread and wine, after those holy words pronounced by the priest becomes the substance of my physical body and my physical blood that was shed on Calvary...*

"When the priest takes the divine words of the Consecration on his lips, words born of LOVE, FROM AN EXCESSIVE LOVE of the Word God MADE FLESH, he has in them the substance of creation, and shortly afterwards he holds in his hands, I mean immediately after the words are pronounced, the substance of redemption, sacrificing me....

"Oh daughter! the priestly ministry is so sublime, and the bodies and souls of those who perform it should be so HOLY....

"In a way, priests carry out the function of the Holy Spirit in the Incarnation" (T.1920).

5

CONCHITA'S MISSION IN THE BOSOM OF THE CHURCH

God's call in the Eucharist

Immediately after Communion today, the Lord said to me, *"In the Eucharist, when you receive Communion, the Lord passes through, for a long time or a short time, leaving his mark on the soul... but in the lofty union I intend, he does not pass through, but rather he stays in a very special way with the soul — forever if the soul does not abandon him"* (T.770).

Holiness for the Eucharist and for the Cross

The Lord said to me at the feet of my Jesus Eucharist, *"I want you to be holy."*

"But how, Lord?"

"By imitating me. Nail your thoughts and your heart to the Cross and to the Eucharist, these two places are where you should live your life... that is where you will find all the perfect spiritual virtues of the highest level. You will find everything there."

(This was when I understood, Father, I do not know how,

but it was in an endless moment, the practical example of all the virtues that were so sublimely given by Jesus on the Cross and in the Eucharist: his generosity, patience, charity, mortification, humility, obedience and many others besides, his strength in helplessness, his resignation and hidden life in the Eucharist, his profound poverty and self-denial.) And the Lord spoke again, *"You need to be made holy, for you will lead an immense chain of souls behind you, souls that will give me glory"* (T.925).

He told me alone, *"Your life is summed up in the Eucharist and the Cross. The soul that embraces the Cross embraces me and the one who bears the Cross bears me. This is why it weighs so little, and the one who loves it loves me.*

"He who loves the Eucharist, daughter, consequently loves the Cross. The way to my Heart is the Cross and the way to my Spirit is my Heart" (T.1008).

The meaning of the grace of the mystical Incarnation lived by Conchita

In Mass today, after Communion, He told me, *"In a way, daughter, you are the altar and the priest at the same time, since you bear within you the most holy VICTIM OF CALVARY and the EUCHARIST, which you can offer constantly to the eternal Father for the salvation of the world. This is the most precious fruit of the great favor I have worked in you, the mystical incarnation in your heart. I have given you the greatest thing in heaven and on earth. I have given myself to you, but for this purpose"* (T.1875).

The Missionaries of the Holy Spirit and the Eucharist

"One of the purposes of these missionaries is to impart the Holy Spirit to souls, to sanctify souls with my Spirit through solid virtue and love. A Missionary of the Holy Spirit should carry out his mis-

sion of sanctifying, directly in the spiritual direction that this world needs so much.

"In order to carry out his mission well, he should be very well versed, pray hard and have constant recourse to the Holy Sacrament. He should spend a long time with God in the Eucharist and the least possible time with the world, unless charity demands otherwise" (T.2816).

Congregations of worshipers of the Blessed Sacrament

"My daughter. The congregations of women and men are meant to provide me with constant worshipers of the Eucharist, in union with Mary and in memory of Mary, in her mysteries of solitude, in the great suffering that crushed her soul from my Ascension till her death.

"Begin this series of worship, feeling in yourself her sufferings, imitating her in her sorrow, consoling yourself with the Eucharist, Mary's only consolation.

"Offer me in your heart, along with the hearts of all your children, saying 'This is my body, this is my blood'... and then after my Ascension, keep on offering me to the Eternal Father: 'This is my body, this is my blood' on behalf of the world" (T.2908).

The works of the Cross

"I am going to tell you a secret today. I created the Works of the Cross especially the Congregations, so that with their love and sacrifice they might help me to pay the Debt of the Eucharist, a precious Debt with the Father and with the Holy Spirit.

"Everything in the world, daughter, is a debt, a debt that should be paid with gratitude. But my debt for the Incarnation, and *above all the debt for the Eucharist, which is renewed constantly and is paid just the same, this has no end."*

"But Lord, if you alone are worth what the Debt is worth, if only you can *buy yourself* and *pay yourself* and even give us the change, then why do you want to join our poor little coins to your gold, when you are both the goldmine and heaven?"

"It is true that I alone pay for myself and satisfy my debt, God to God, but it is a duty — I am the head and my mystical body participates in the debt, and, since it participates in my grace and in the Eucharist, it is obliged to do so. But there is more — it is because of the victim's love for the Victim, honor, gratitude and more heaven. It is to console me, to be united to the One God *and to participate in his debts and in his pearls.*

"Are pearls not pain for the soul that loves me? And why? Because the lover tends to be like the Beloved, and if I am in debt, then the loving soul should also want to be in debt to me, to be in debt to God....

This is so sublime, my daughter! To buy me and to pay me, and how? What more perfect way could you find in heaven or on earth than by saying together with me 'This is my body, this is my blood, beloved Father, divine Spirit!' Payment is thus made by loving, by being transformed in the unity" (T.2917).

Conchita's eucharistic mission

"Your role, daughter, is that of a Mass mystically continued, and such should be the role of the Oases, to continue the offering, offering me to the Father, and offering themselves with me.... So many forget me, daughter! So many offend me! But the mission of the Oases is to repair this forgetfulness in union with Mary, consoling me, remembering me, but in the way I have told you.

"You see, I am hurt more by forgetfulness than by the world's offenses, because I am forgotten by my own people, and this deeply wounds my sensitive Heart.

"Do not forget me, and may your people not forget me, because forgetting implies ingratitude, and this is the worst thorn in my Heart.

"Remember me by offering me, because if you remember me you remember the Father; you will remember both of us together.

"If only you could see how much forgetfulness there is of my Divine Person and of my graces among my own people!" (T.3076).

Conchita's priestly mission

"And so, during the hours of these crucifying Masses will my soul be ceaselessly loving and consoling you day and night, covering you with tenderness and caressing you, repairing with you the offenses suffered by your heavenly Father?"

"Yes, Concha, for yours is a priestly mission, and together with Mary you will know not only how to console me but also to save them. Does your soul not desire to love me endlessly? Today I am placing in your soul this means of glorifying me, atoning with love.... Love, as I have told you, is the great atonement, the great repairer, and what is there that cannot be accomplished by maternal love, by the fullness of the Third Love?" (T.3403.a).

"Lord, would you like to explain to me how my soul can be present in every Mass, as you told me yesterday?"

"It is very simple. Inasmuch as you are transformed into me, wherever I am, you are, and wherever you are, I am, because of this unifying union that makes one out of two.

"You will be in the Masses together with Mary through the reflection of the divine motherhood, by reason of the Mystical Incarnation in your soul and as a fortunate result of this grace.

"You will be there with your will, a power superior to the soul, which together with mine forms just one desire with mine.

"You will be present through love, which is everywhere and bridges all distances, which climbs up to heaven and reaches the infinite bosom of God, who is One and yet many.

"You will be present, because this is my Will, and that is sufficient.

"But apart from this, my intention is that your mind will never be separated from me, as far as this is possible, that your memory will always be with me, that your tenderness and consolation of the Third Love continue in your soul and that I will never be without them. My intention is that your soul be joined together with that of Mary, as a sign of your union with her, fulfilling your mission on the altars.

You already know your mission — it consists of adoring, atoning and consoling my Heart, obtaining graces for priests glorifying me" (T.3404).

Father, can you see what I feel? Can it be that Jesus' words are being fulfilled? I can feel my soul present at Mass all over the world, in intimate and constant remembrance of Jesus. It is not just a normal remembrance, but a memory with life — a living and intimate remembrance, as if the remembrance of him who calls me and my own remembrance that follows him met on the way.

It is a memory of *possession* — I have it and I want to have it. It is as if the memory were his image, as if it were he himself, and day and night I think of the altar on which he is constantly sacrificed, and I see myself next to him, offering him up with Mary. His memory is he himself for me; it is both possession and union.

My love for Mary is also growing day by day, as if her perfection and virtue were illuminating me, as if she were drawing me to herself with trust, and I do not run away at the point of shame because of the Mystical Incarnation, but rather I fall into her arms, asking her for her lessons of love (T.3405).

In union with Mary, the co-redeemer

"This is your role, to be present with your soul together with my Mother at Mass.… Does your soul not sigh and weep when you see insulting and sacrilegious Masses, even though your body is not there?

"This place on the altar belongs to you because of this maternal detail, because, Concha, Mary's Son is also your Son (Oh, God!), the Son of your heart, the one who is crucified on the altar by both worthy and unworthy priests, and your motherly soul has to be present to weep and to suffer, to love and console, or to be joyful when the Immaculate Lamb is offered to the Father by pure hands.…

"My sacrifice would not be complete without my Mother's heart, because of Mary's motherhood. She completed my Passion, and she keeps on carrying out her role as co-redemptrix.

"The Church, together with its priests and its faithful, should continue my Passion on earth.

"The favor I have bestowed on you with these exercises, C., is very great — joining you to Mary in a special way…" (T.3406).

At night I felt a painful sorrow inside, and I remembered him offended in so many Masses. Jesus came without my asking him, and he told me this, *"You see, spiritual fatherhood or motherhood obtains grace, since its intercession, because of its divine origin, is more powerful.*

"God gives himself continuously, and motherly souls *should also give* themselves. *But where do they receive if not from the eternal Fountain of all graces?*

"This is why their spirits have to be joined like the runners to the Vine" (T.3406.a).

"But that is my role on earth, the mission of a Man-God's most purified love, to live constantly on earth as a sacrifice on the altars reliving the Passion of Calvary, to enable them to reach heaven.

"The sacrifice of the Cross on the altar was enough, but the cruelty of my wicked priests has led me to another Calvary on the

73

same altar — *another sacrifice, another Passion, double martyrdom with the sacrilege they impose on me, a double Cross on which they doubly sacrifice me, on which they challenge heaven and my very Person, not only laden with their sins but as if* I were the actual criminal.

"*And what happens next? Mary comes in between her two sons, interceding to heaven and obtaining forgiveness, sacrificing her only Son with this delicate motherly martyrdom.*

"*And this concerns you and all motherly souls. They alone have this privilege. The Father listens to them and they appease him, because there is a holy thread of fruitfulness in those same motherly souls (because of the Mystical Incarnation), and this is wherein the secret of their power for intercession lies, because in a way God sees God in them, the Father sees the Father, from the same holy thread of motherhood received from the Father.*"

"But sacrificing the holy and pure Son is martyrdom, Jesus of my soul, in order to obtain forgiveness for the other guilty and pitiless son, who dares to be you, and together with you to offend your Father."

"*But once again, this is my role, the role of the sacrificed Lamb, and your role and Mary's is the one of motherly martyrdom, offering up in the same way as the Father the Divine Son to be crucified, but with this unheard-of difference.*

"*My enemies did not know what they were doing on Calvary, but my wicked priests crucify me twice on the altar, fully aware of their betrayal and shamelessness, and they martyr me with a double martyrdom, the martyrdom of seeing myself in them, a criminal before my Father, and the martyrdom of drinking from the chalice of their condemnation, a very delicate and painful martyrdom for my soul that loves them so much.*

"*And this double martyrdom also implies a double love, the love that you should have on the altar, the tremendous pain of seeing me doubly sacrificed by my wicked priests, and the awful torture of seeing the treacherous priest condemned in life. Rather than with a kiss, he betrays me to such terrible suffering and to a double*

pain, the pain of seeing myself offending my Father in the priest,
together with what he most loves, his own Son, *who only wants*
endless worship for him, and the pain of seeing the Savior of the world
as a reproach to the priest until he is washed with contrition, that
is, with my blood, *the same blood that he has drunk sacrilegiously.*

"*Can you see your role more clearly now on many of my al-*
tars?" (T.3423).

Satan's attacks on Conchita's mission

Satan's violent attacks are terrible and his sarcasm freezes
the soul! A voice said to me, "What have you done in these exercises that will only obtain for you hell or centuries of purga-
tory? Invent... praise yourself... deceive... be wearisome and
annoying... waste time and make others waste it too.

"What practical fruit have you obtained other than ridicu-
lous illusions? You should be more humble, a surer path, but
you are stupidly trying to fly.

"And now, these heights with Mary! What a nerve! How
rude! This is the height of arrogance, with that feigned motherhood.

"All your flights of arrogance in these exercises are nothing more than infamy! They are stupidities — someone your age
should know better!

"Learn to scorn yourself, get ready to die well and get rid
of this nonsense and these things that harm your soul.

"It is deceit, iniquity and a bad example, one after another,
that you are struggling under for all eternity!

"It is an insult to Jesus! You are unbelievably daring with
his Eternal Majesty!

"Putting yourself on a par with Mary!

"Going to Mass with all those absurd ideas!

"Asking favors for others so insolently!

"Thinking with such incredible arrogance that you receive grace, and that whatever you ask heaven for will be granted!"

(And I felt, Father, a sarcasm that froze me, and tears welled up in my eyes, and without being able to reply and without wanting it my soul was confused, and here you have me on rugged terrain, surrounded by clouds and storms, with terrible thunder inside me, and I only feel consolation and peace by humbling myself, and I do not wish to leave the ground.)

Oh my God! Oh Father!

I told my confessor everything and he calmed me down, but an immense weight oppressed my soul and a deep pain filled me.

My tears were falling at the feet of Jesus, and he said to me, *"It was necessary for the dew of your tears to accompany your requests. Be in peace."*

("That peace is false" the other voice said.) But my confessor told me that even when the devil attacked me in that way, I should ask Jesus for a kiss and not listen. This is what I will do (T.3408).

Thanksgiving for the Eucharist in the foundations

WHAT A GREAT DAY IT IS TODAY! Happy anniversary! 25 years of perpetual exposure day and night in the Houses of the Cross.

All the Houses of the Cross celebrated a *day of love*, with thanksgiving all day long. Our hearts were overflowing with gratitude — what would the Oasis be without the Eucharist? It could not exist.

The Eucharist is the divine driving force, the gatherer of love, the central point of the life of the Sisters of the Cross, their happiness, their purity, their strength, their rest, their direction, their desire, the realized ideal of their vocation.

Oh my Jesus Eucharist, blessed art thou!

Thank you, my Jesus, and may the years and centuries pass by, may the end of the world come and find the Sisters of the Cross worshiping you in your Sacrament of love, atoning, begging with their voluntary sacrifices, consoling your Heart of love.

Oh Jesus, Jesus of all my soul! I want to fly to you, hang round your neck a thousand times and more, love you... be overwhelmed... sacrifice myself... conquer myself... melt in your divine love giving you my soul, my body and a thousand lives if I had them!

I want to love you and I cannot love you, I want to be good and I cannot. It is as if I were on a sharp ledge that stops me and I weep, and my soul sighs as if it had been abandoned, and I have nowhere to put my stained, weary and hurting heart.

It is martyrdom to be among people, it is distress to be alone, I am frozen among roses, I am distracted in prayer, I am *alone* everywhere.

Oh Lord of my soul! What was the Third Love? An illusion? Arrogance? It seems like they were different people back then, and reality is what I am experiencing now. I cast this aside as a temptation, but Oh Lord! Give me faith, give me hope, give me love, that Charity which burns everything, sets everything alight right down to the straw of imperfection (T.3436).

ST PAULS

This book was produced by St. Pauls/Alba House, the Society of St. Paul, an international religious congregation of priests and brothers dedicated to serving the Church through the communications media.

For information regarding this and associated ministries of the Pauline Family of Congregations, write to the Vocation Director, Society of St. Paul, P.O. Box 189, 9531 Akron-Canfield Road, Canfield, Ohio 44406-0189. Phone (330) 702-0396; or E-mail: spvocationoffice@aol.com or check our internet site, www.albahouse.org